Coloring book for adults and kids amazing horse image for design

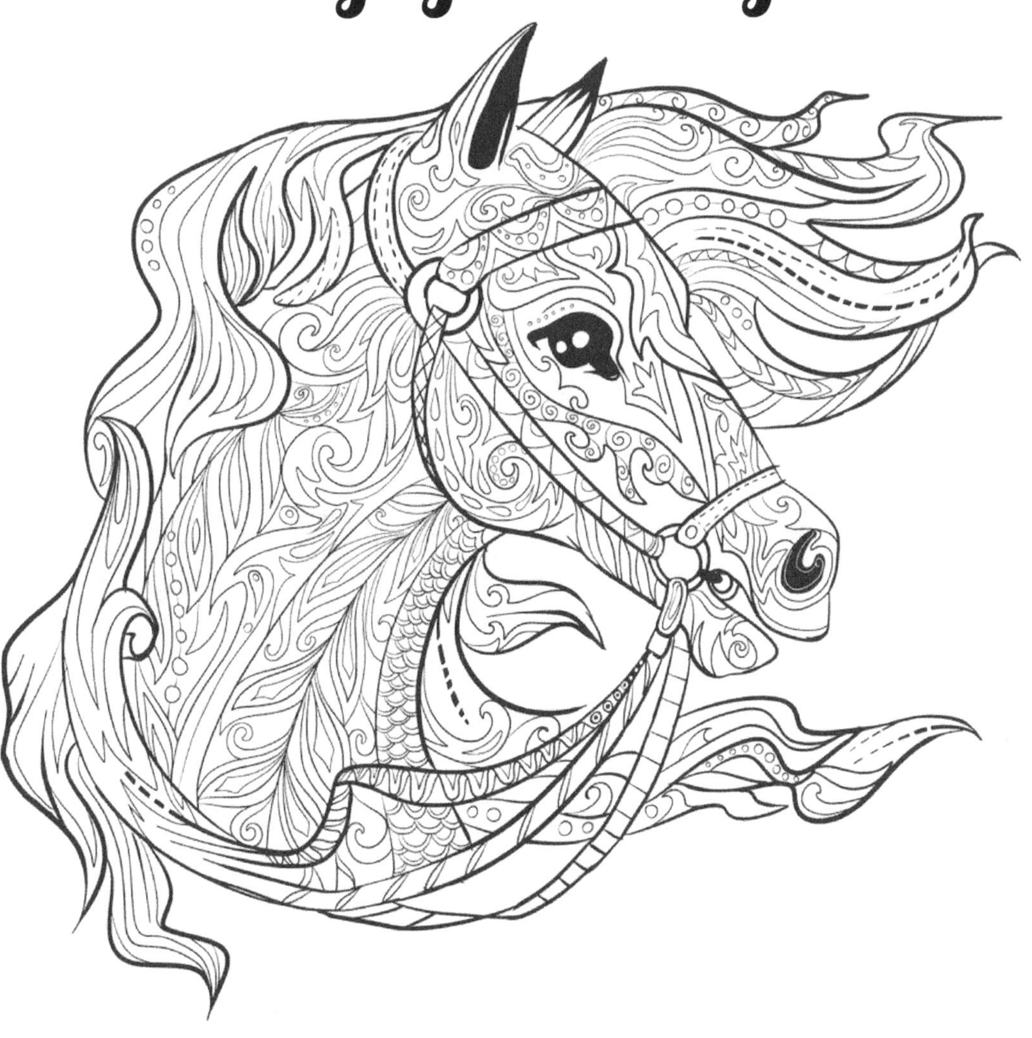

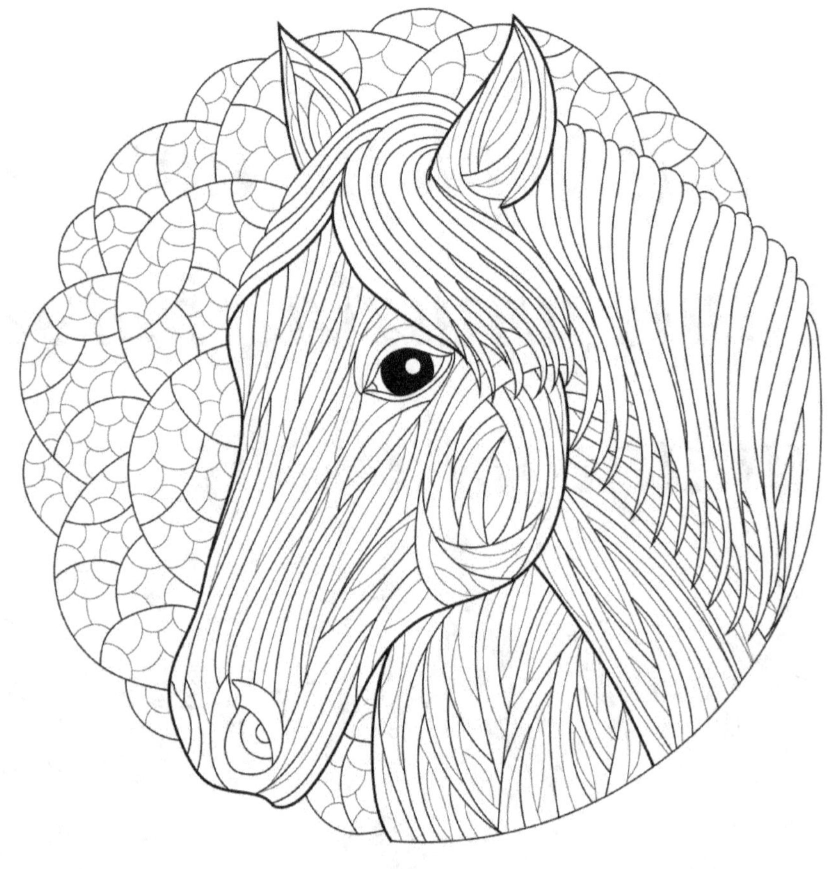

This book is belongs to

____

____

____

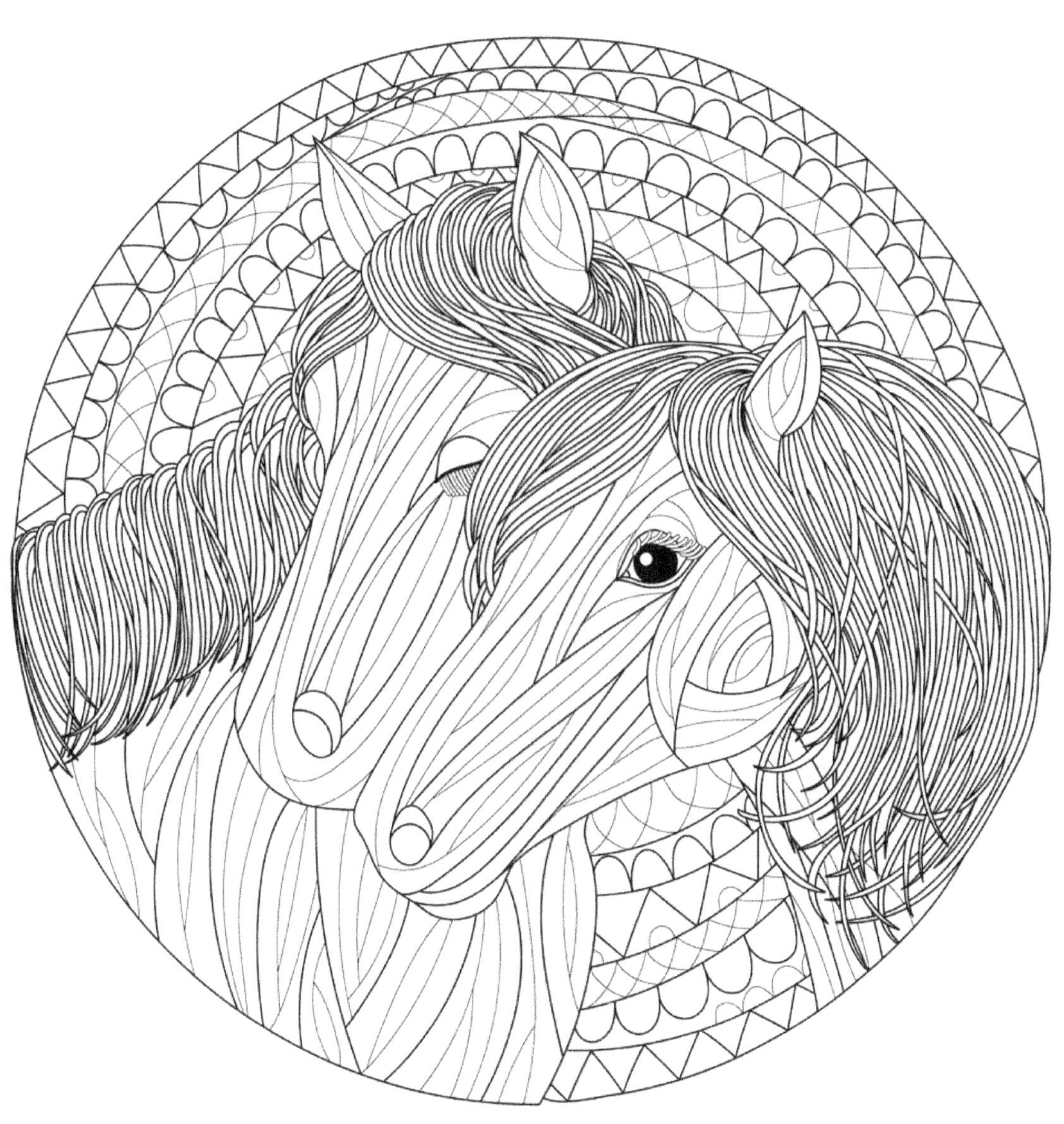

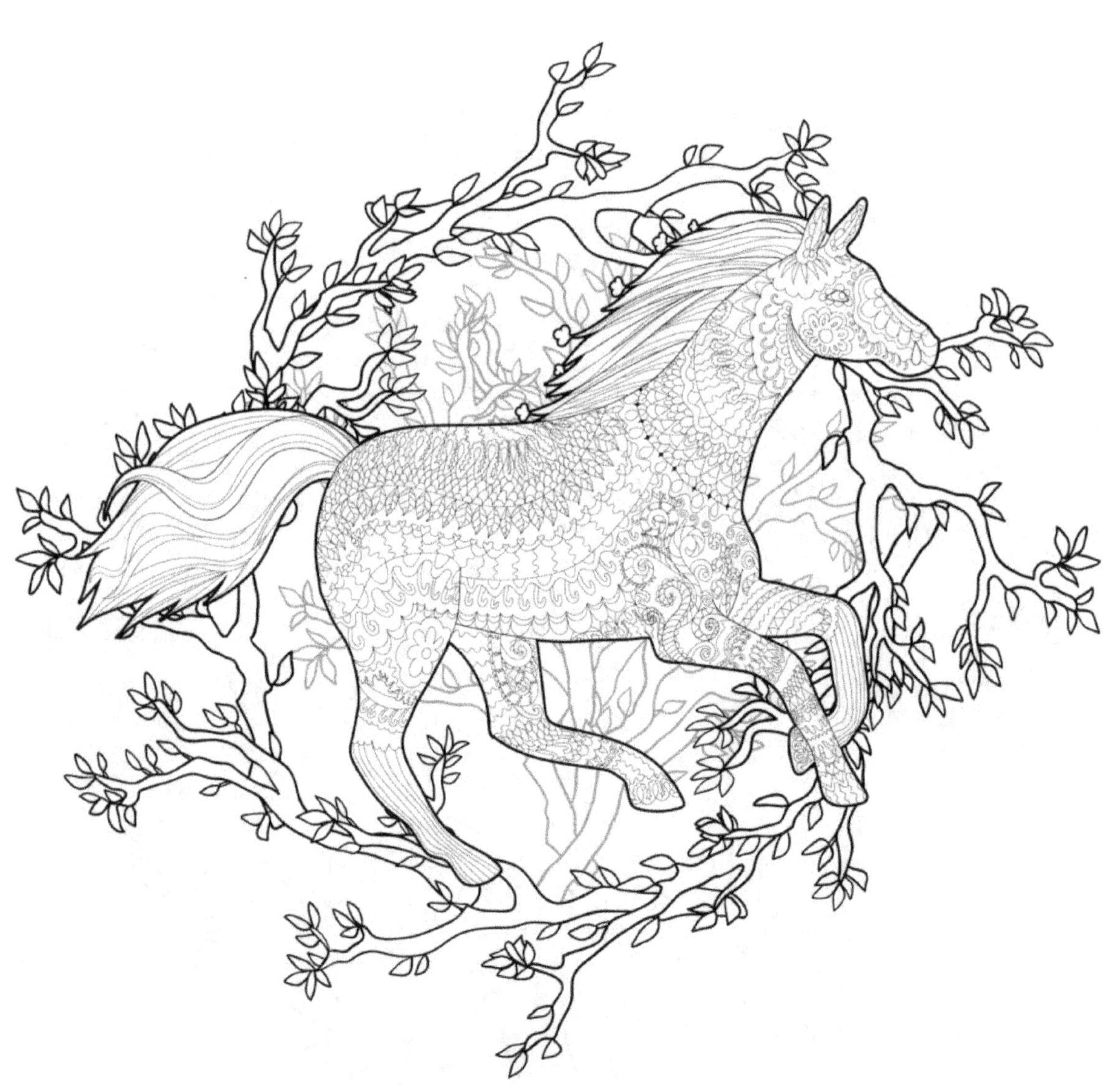

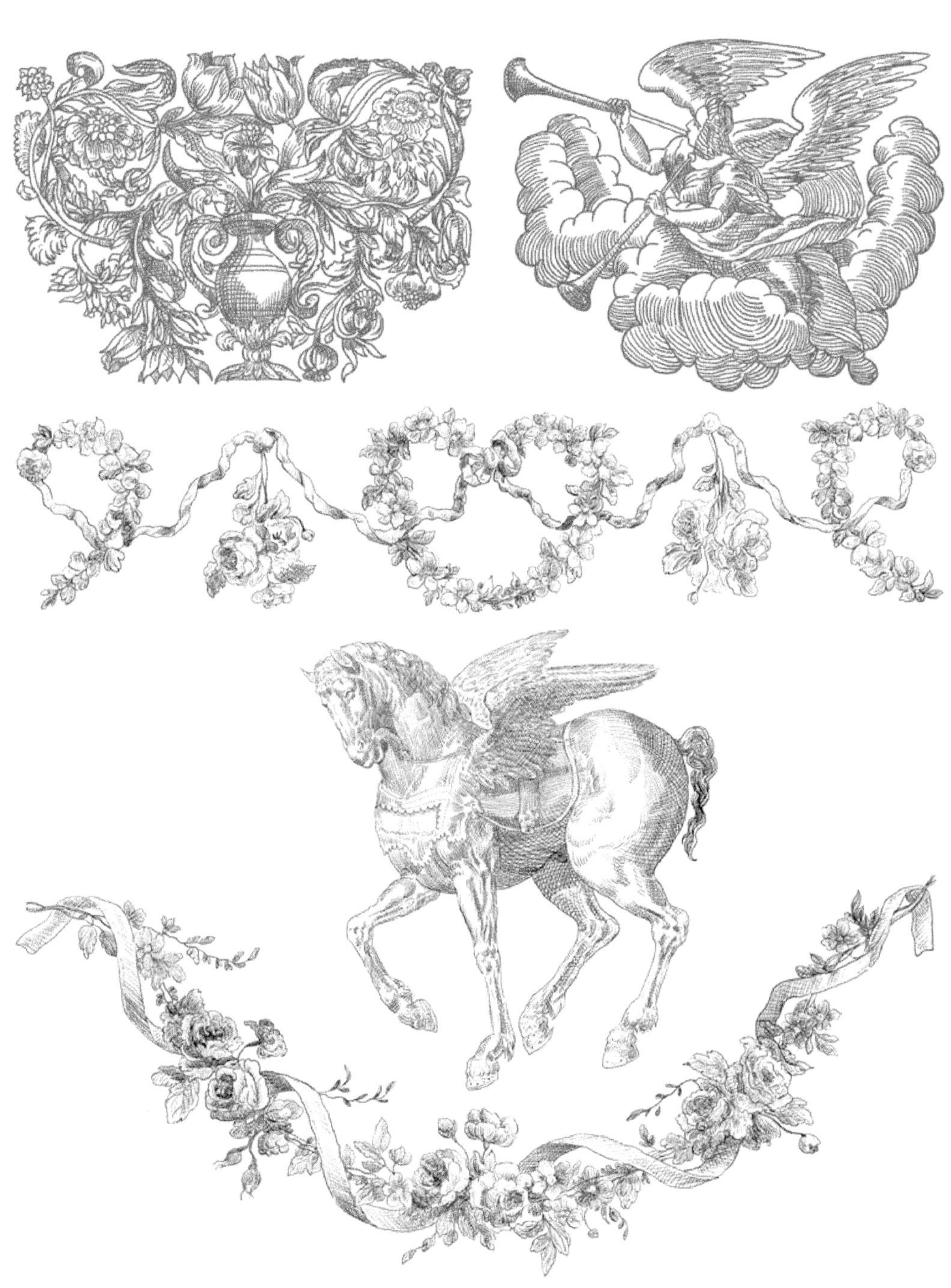

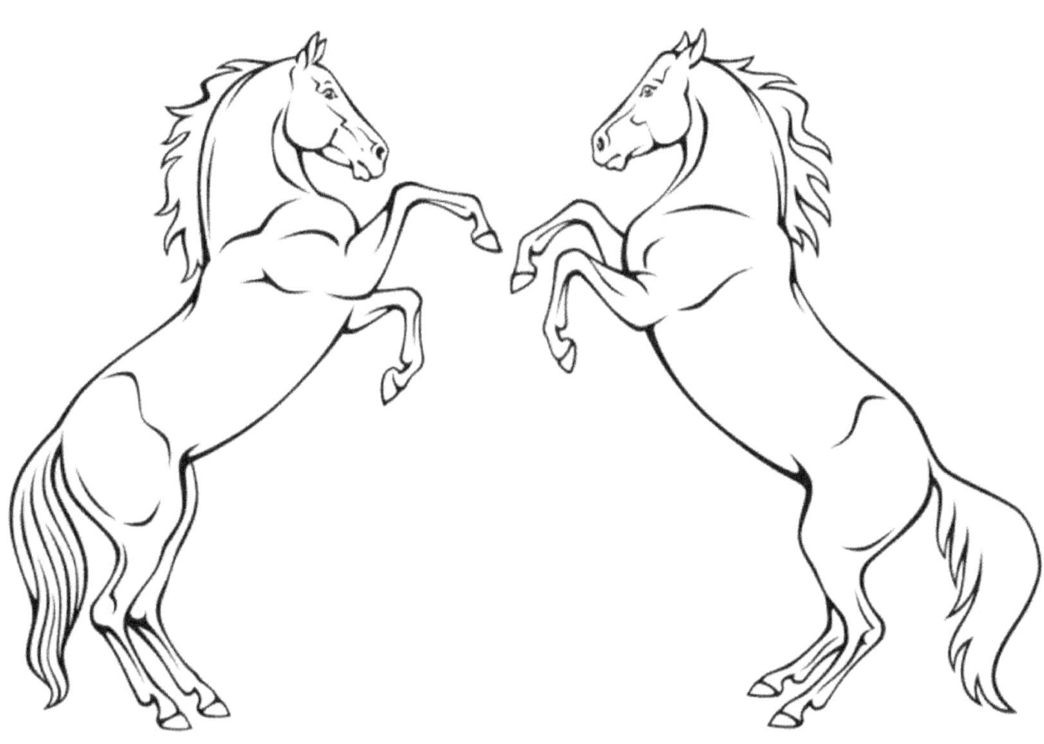

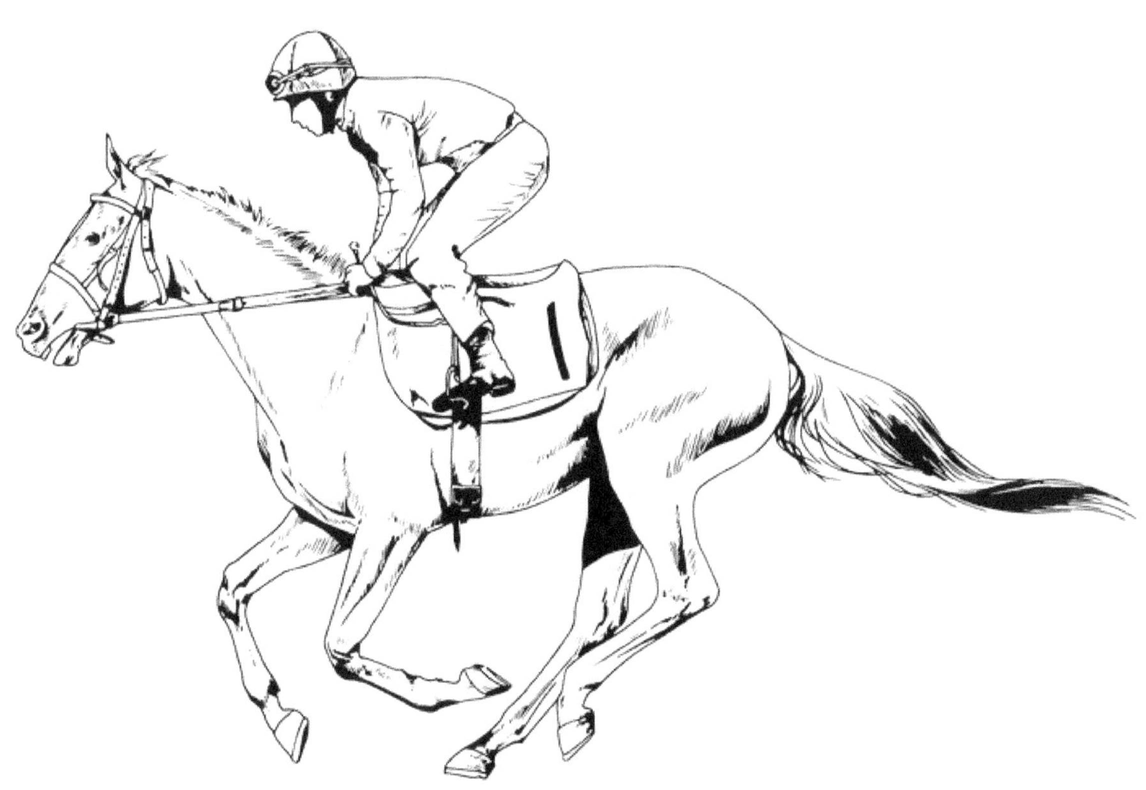

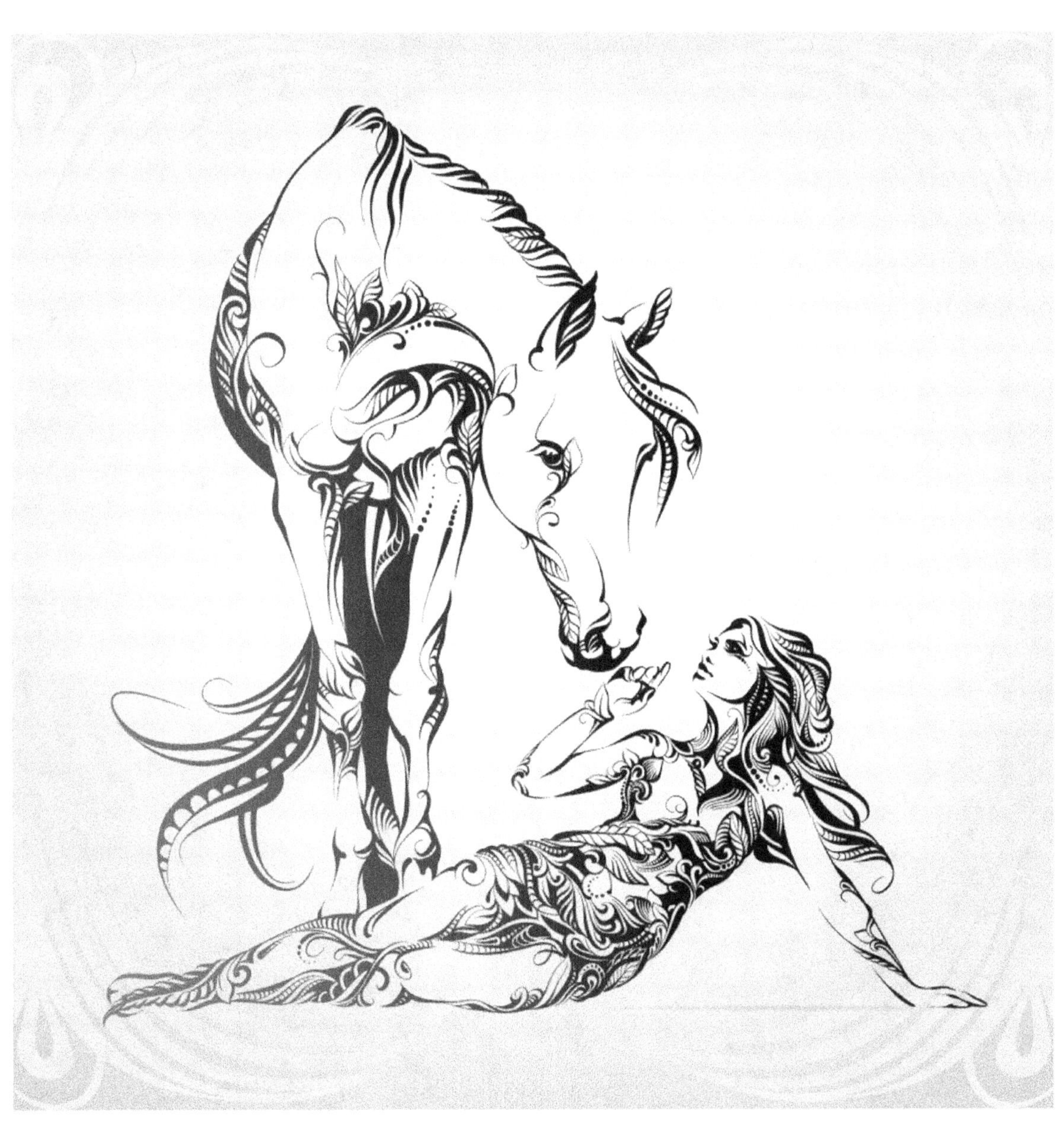

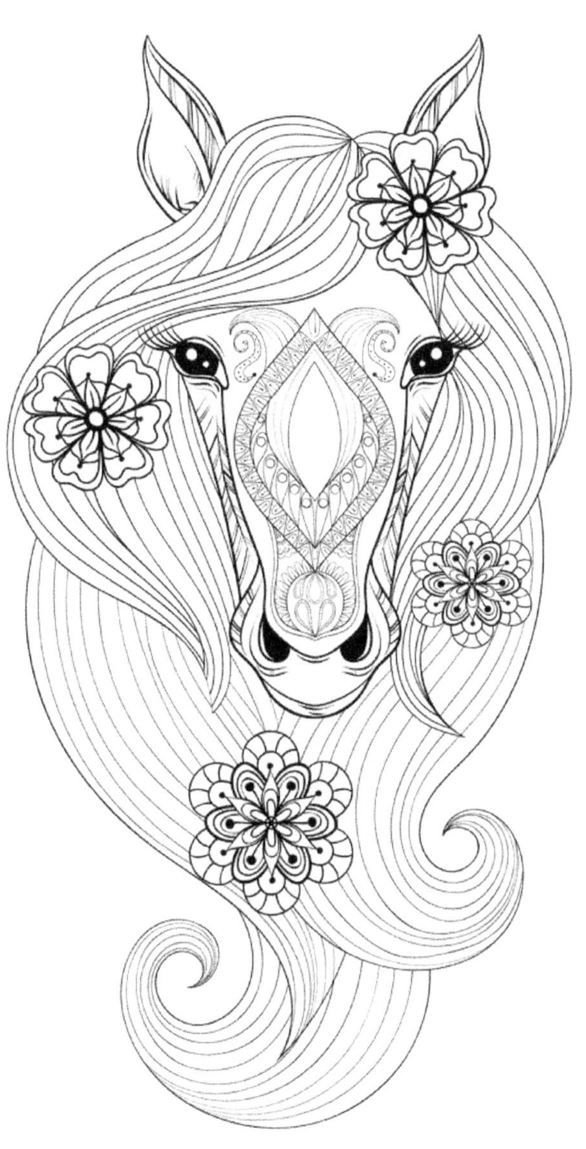

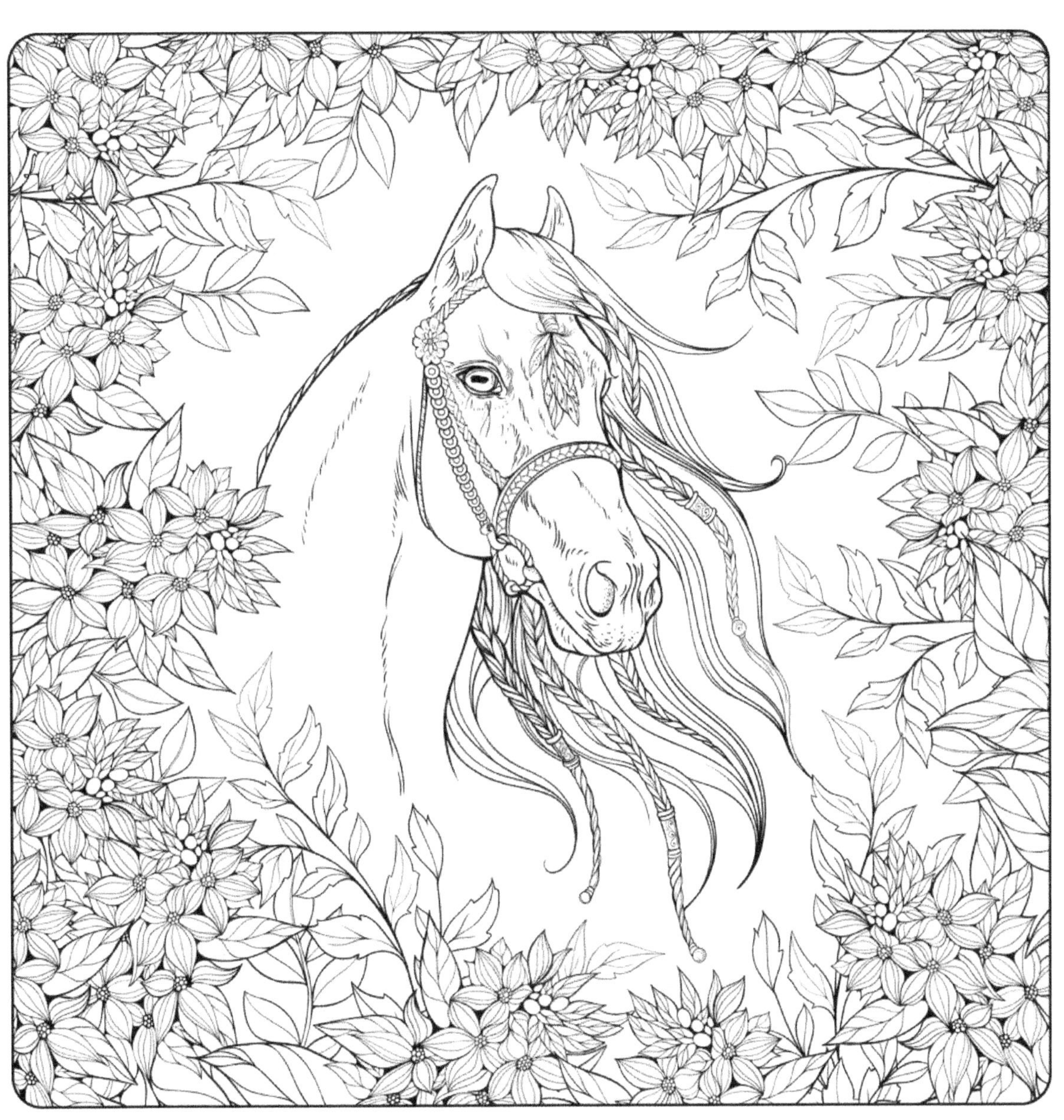

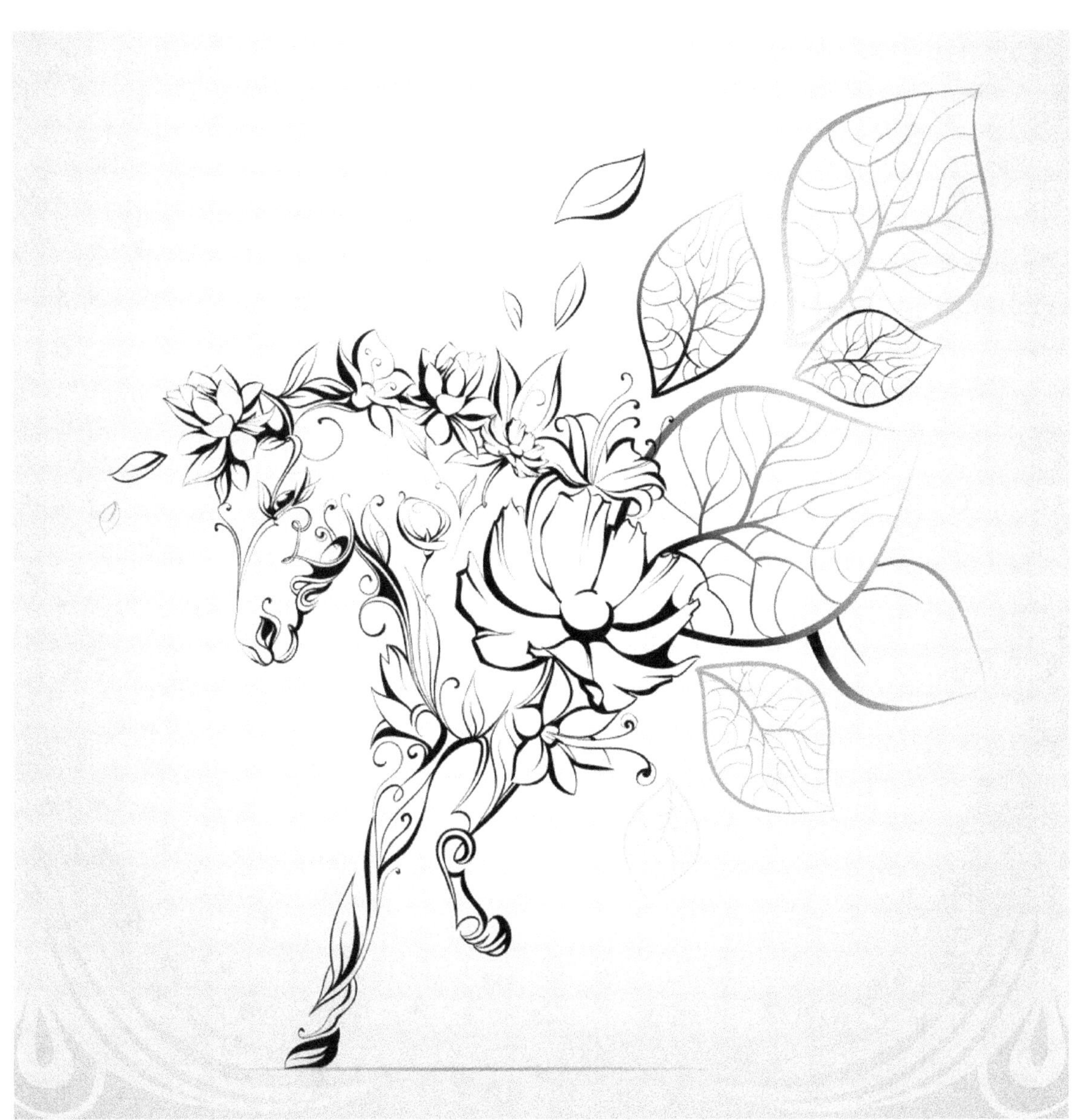

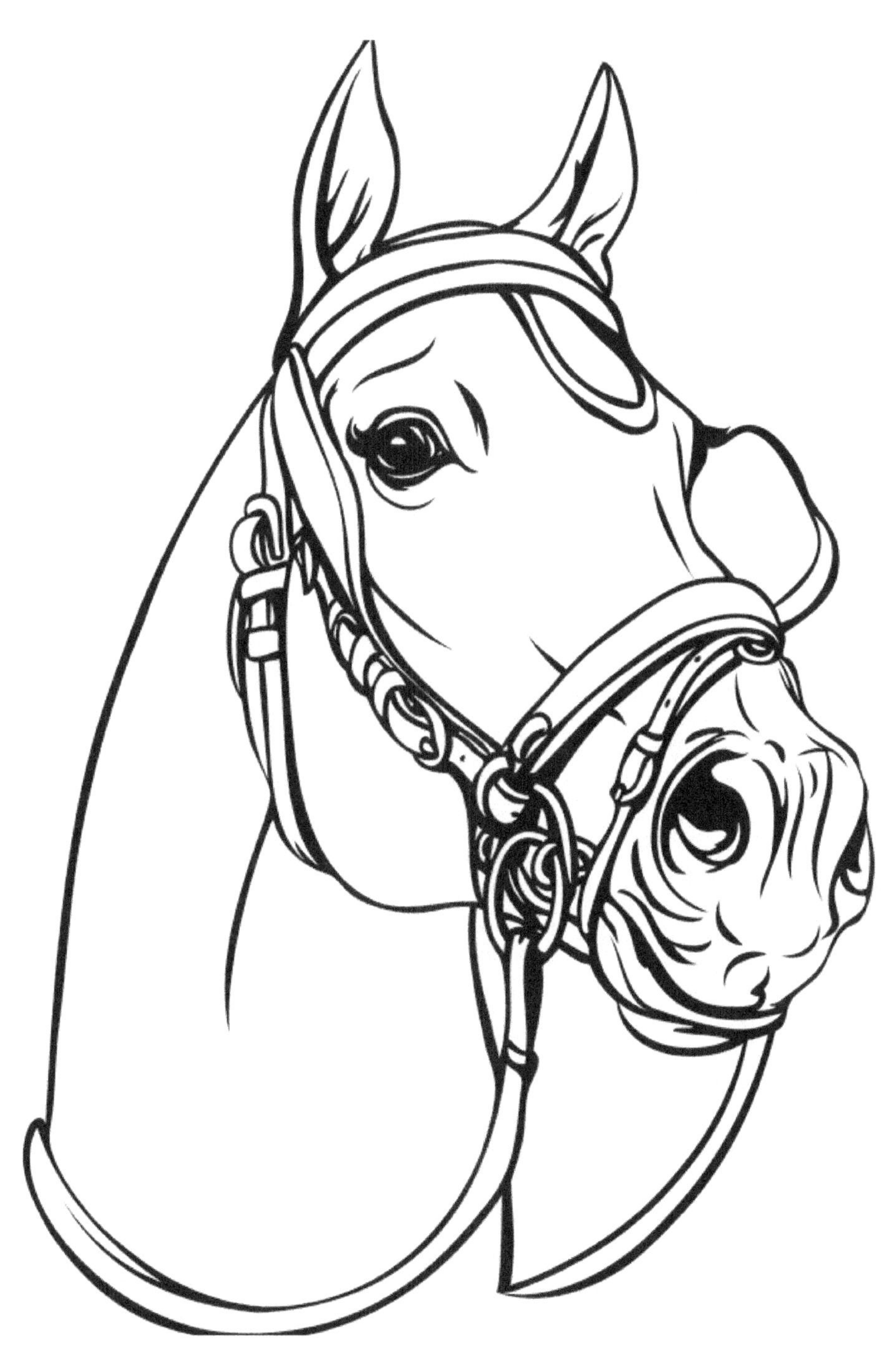

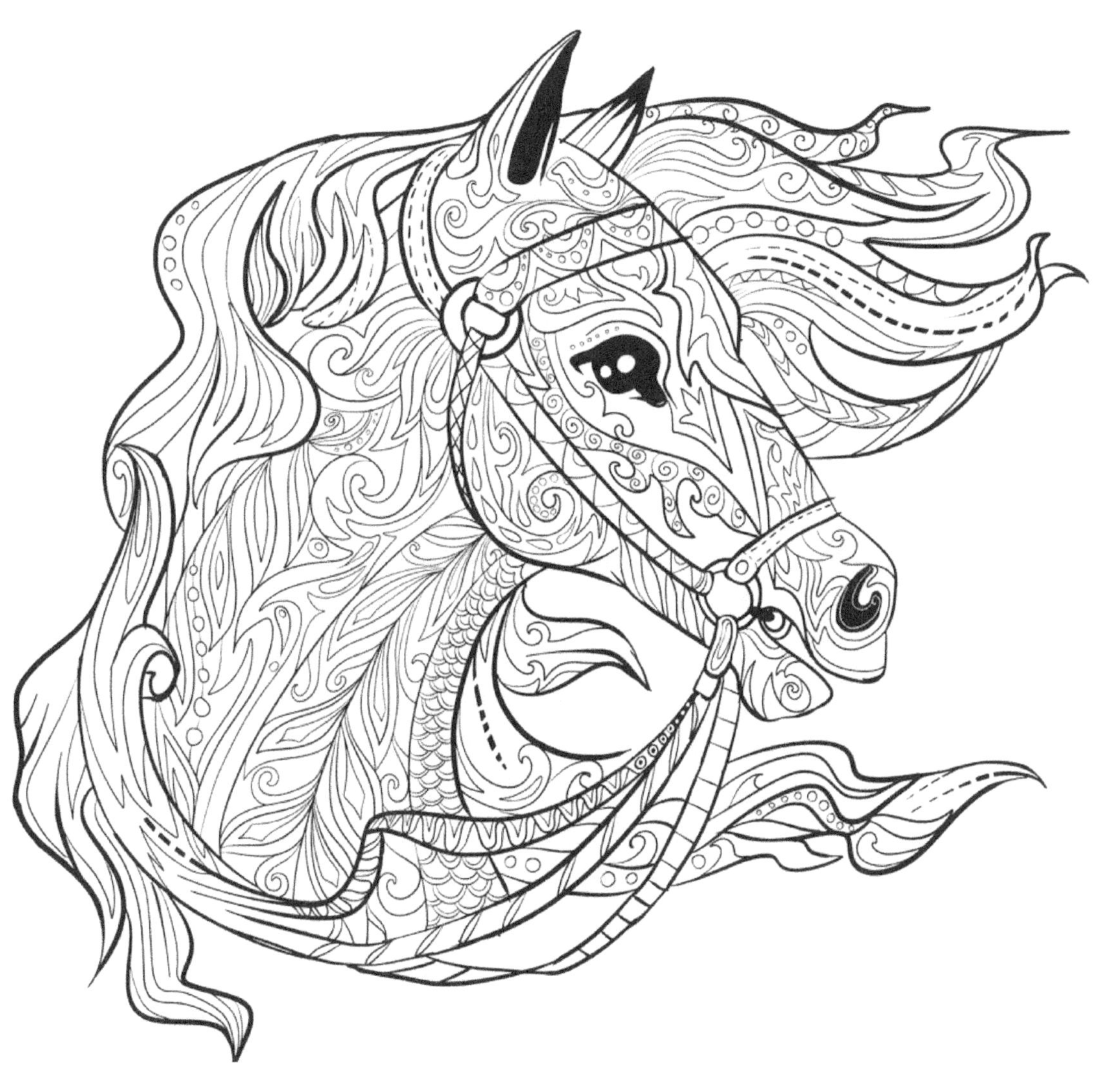

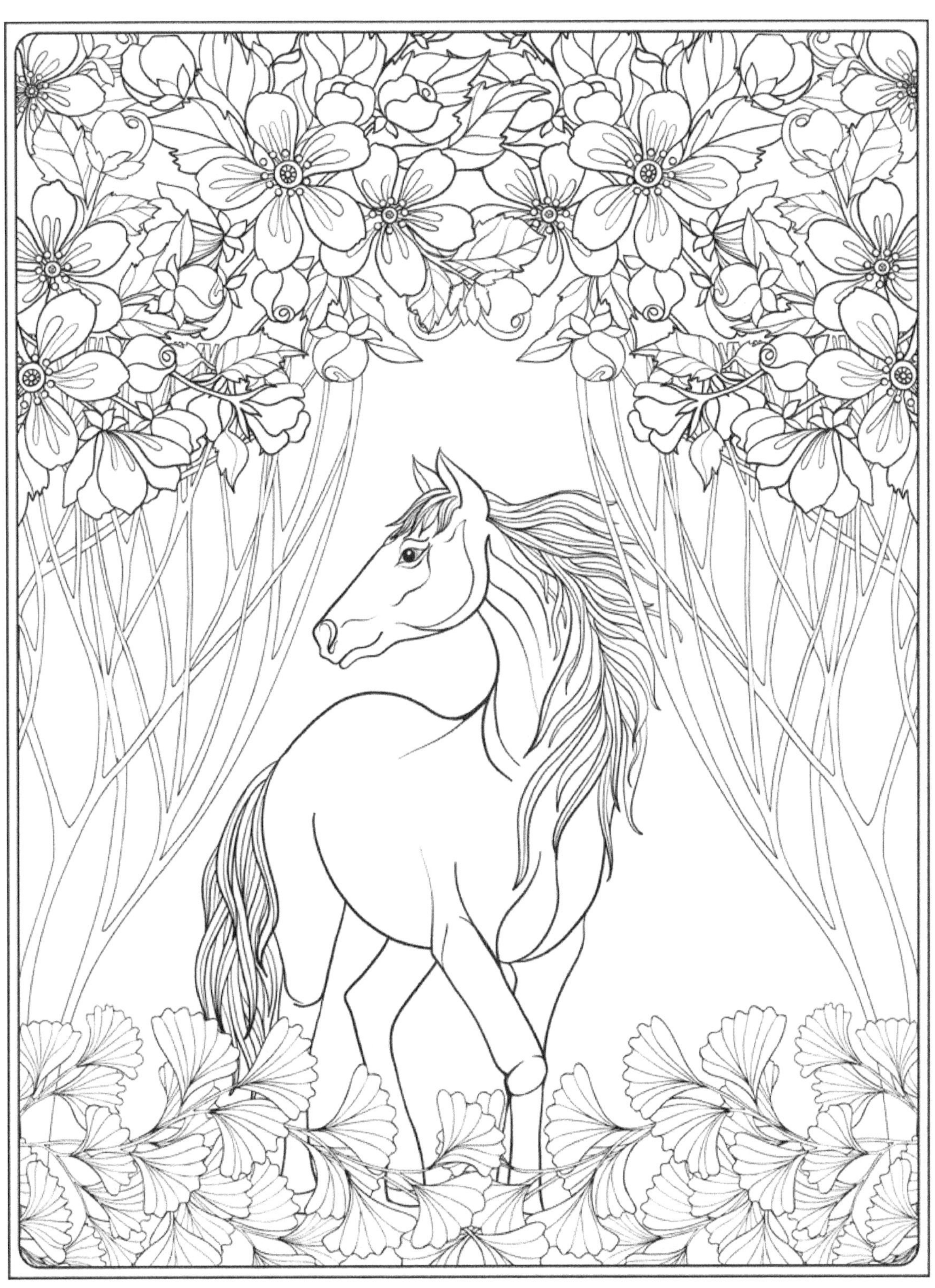

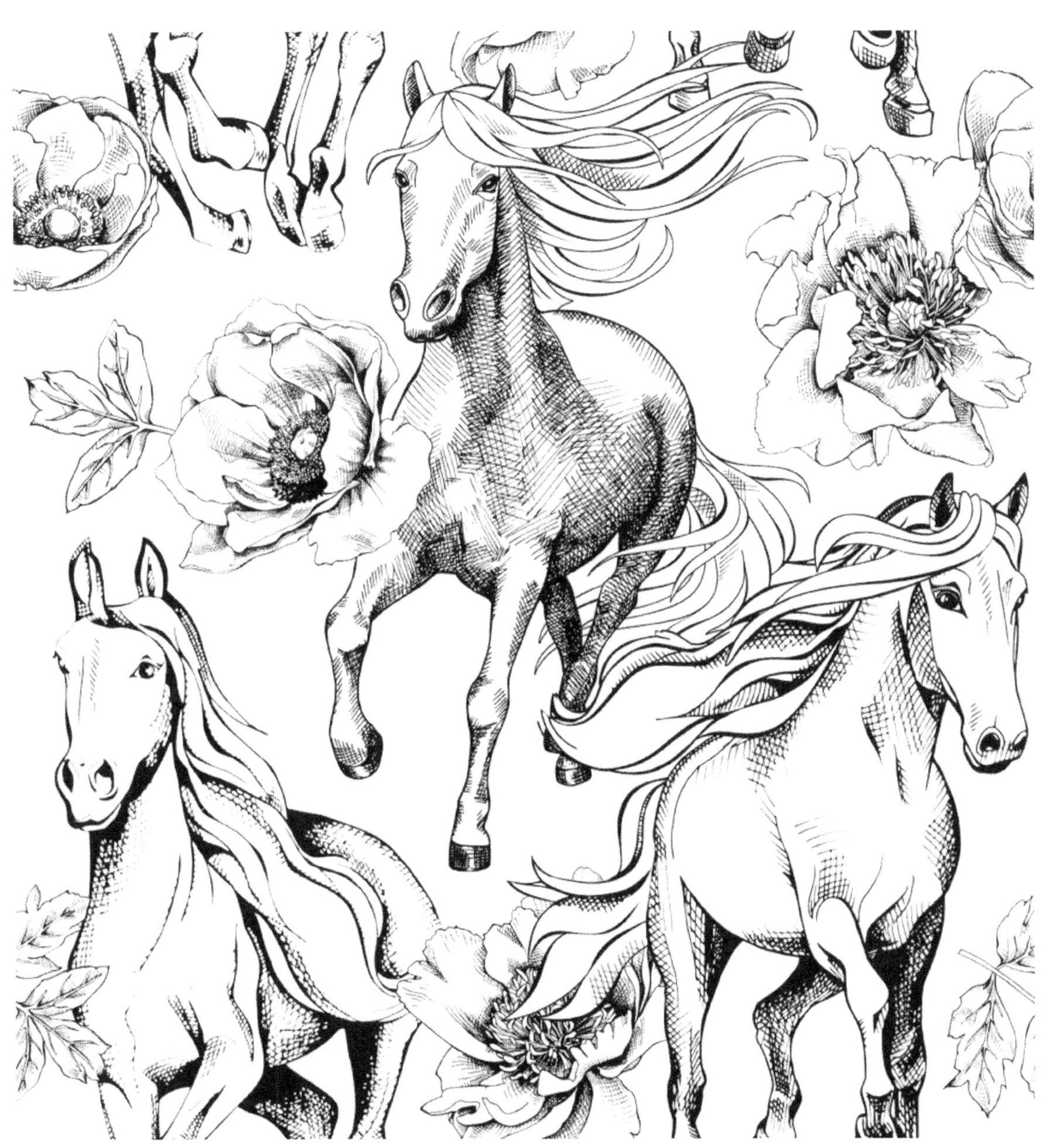

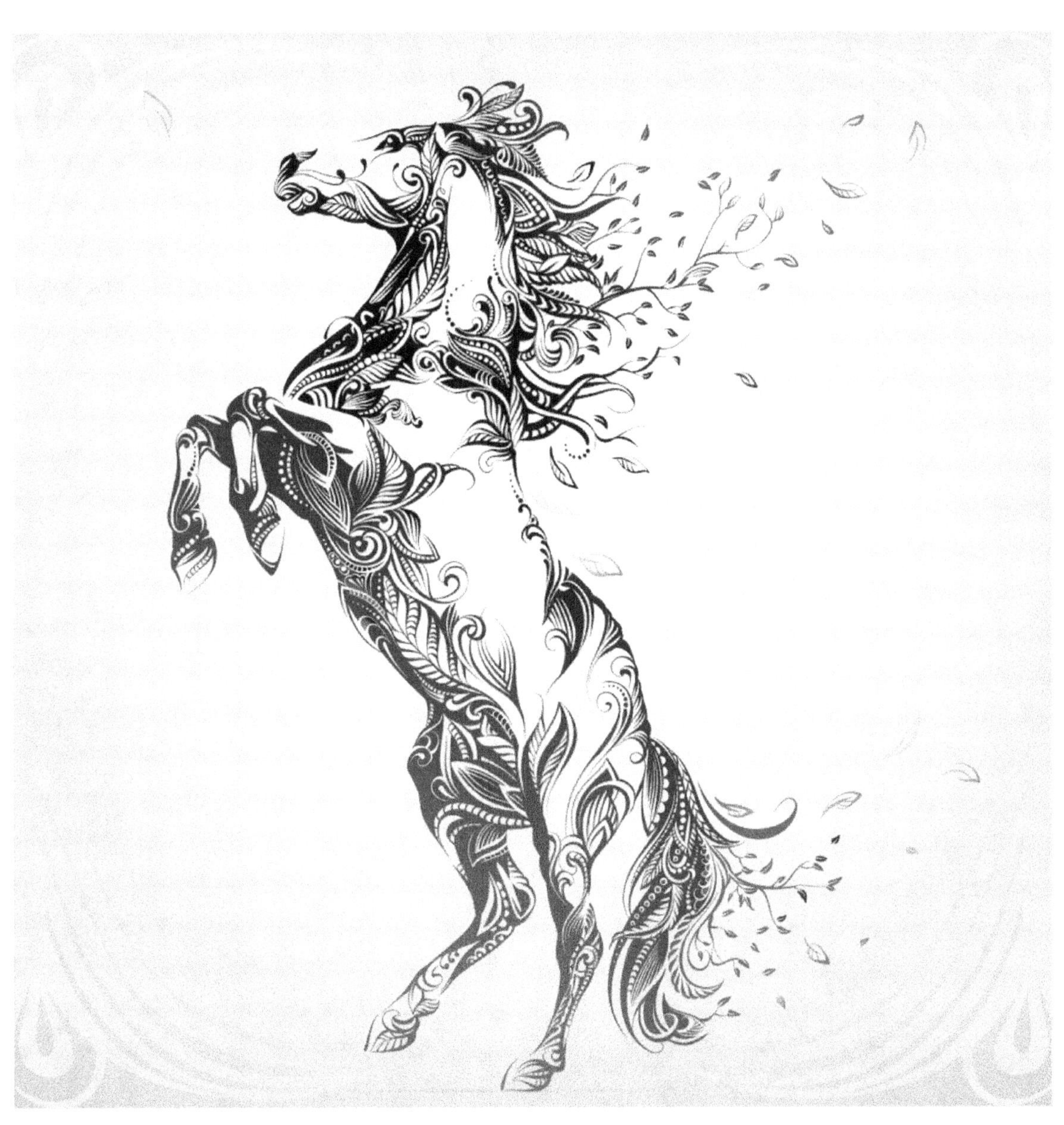

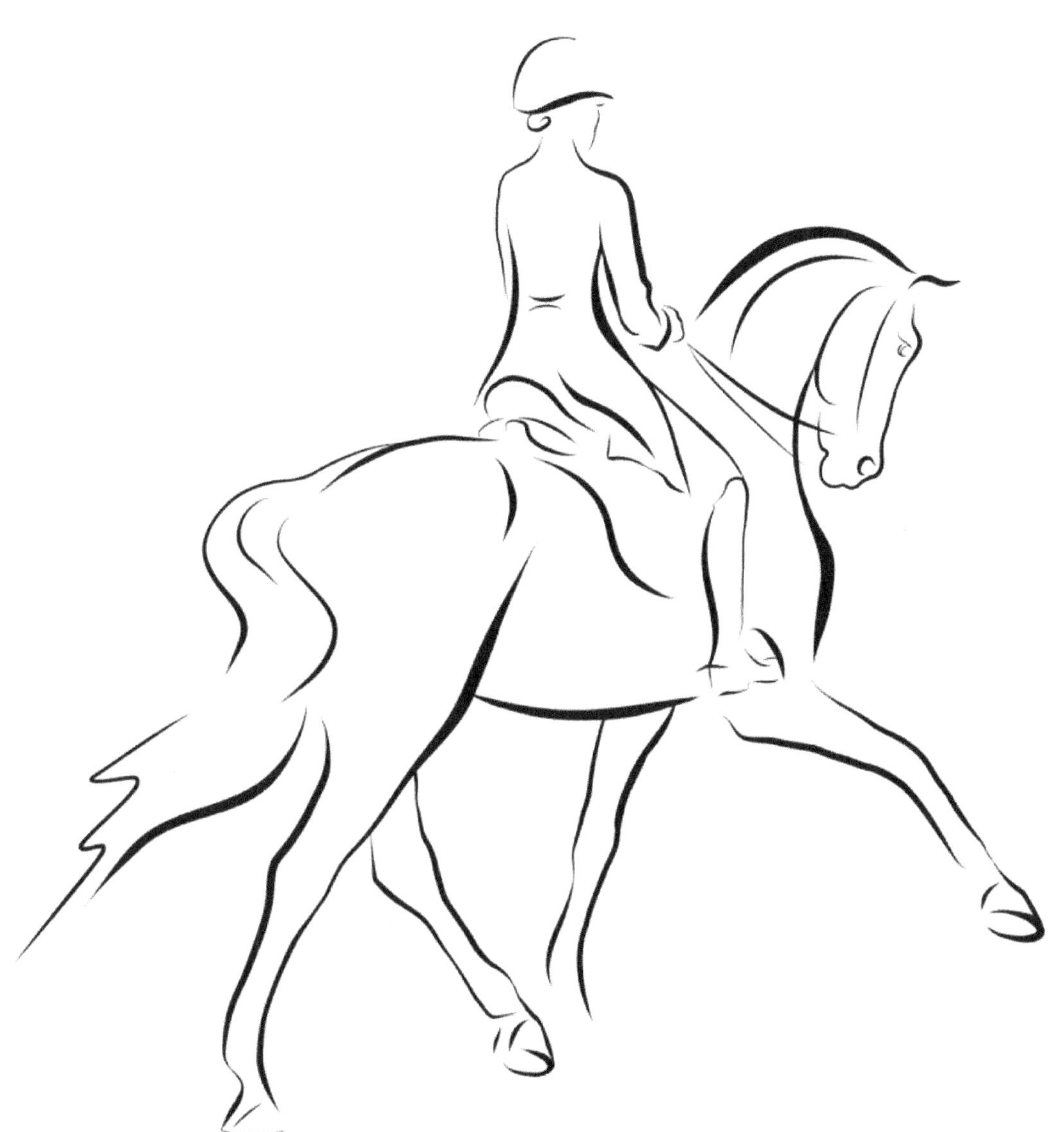

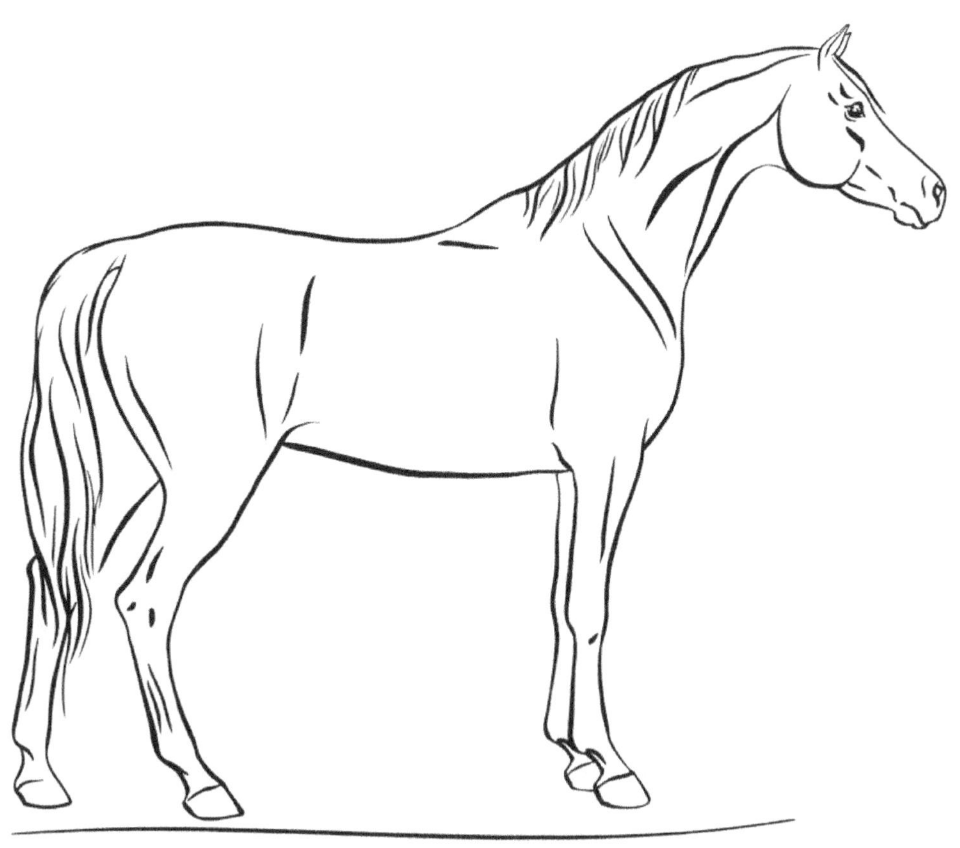

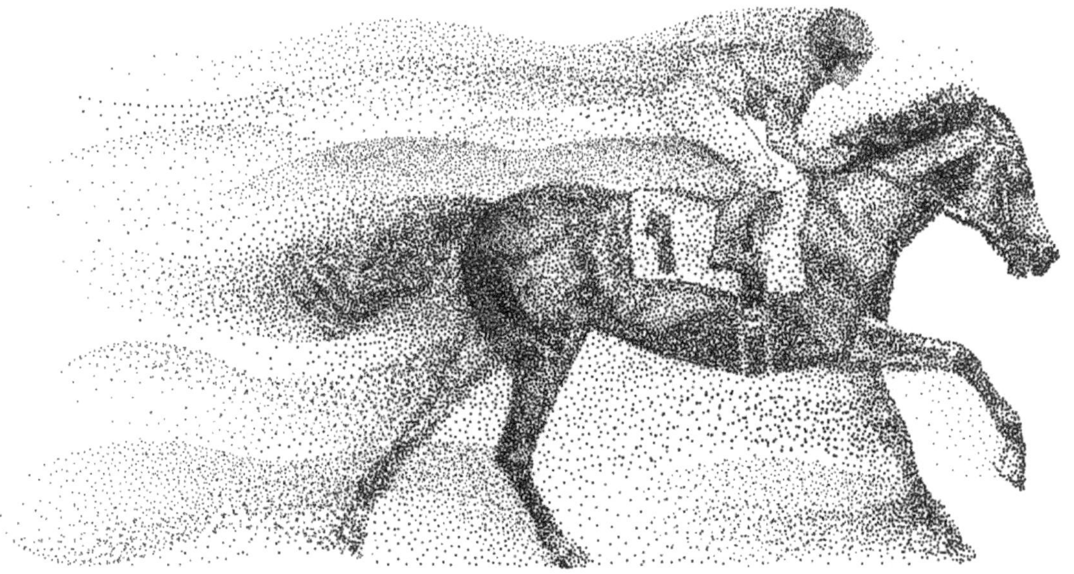

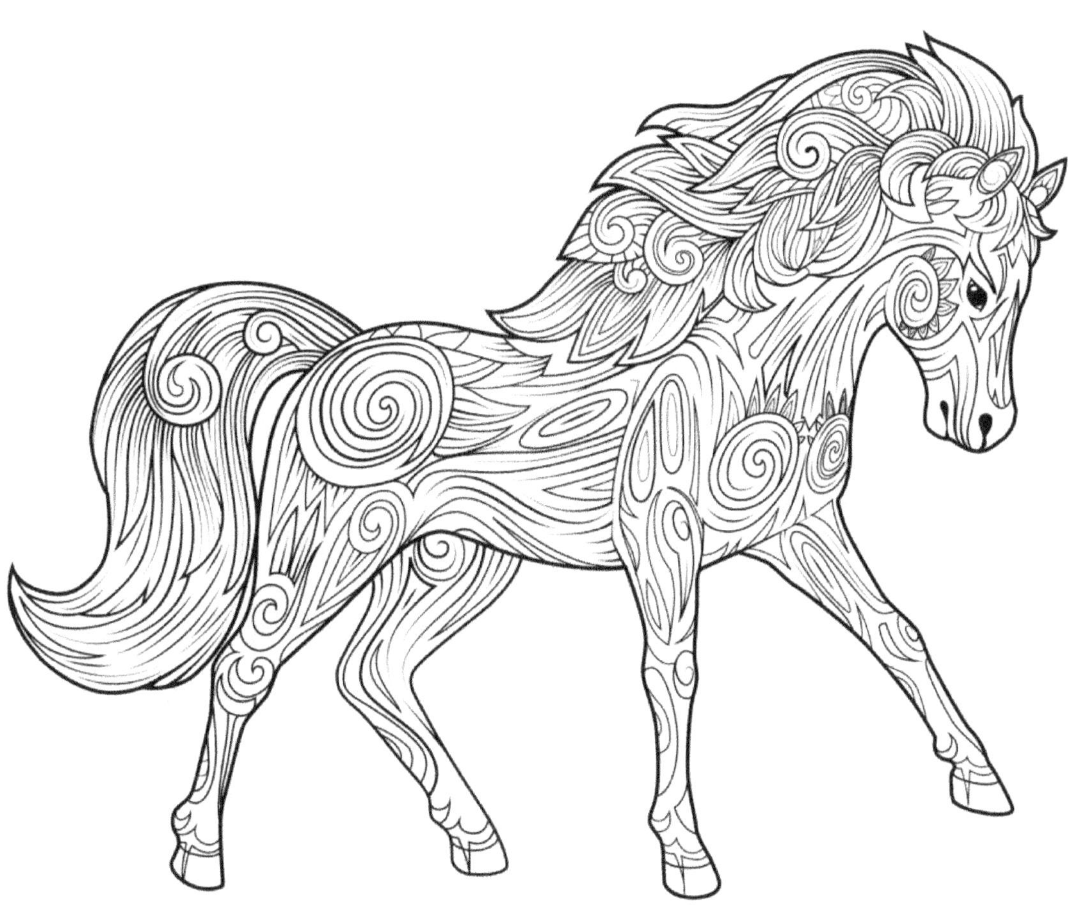

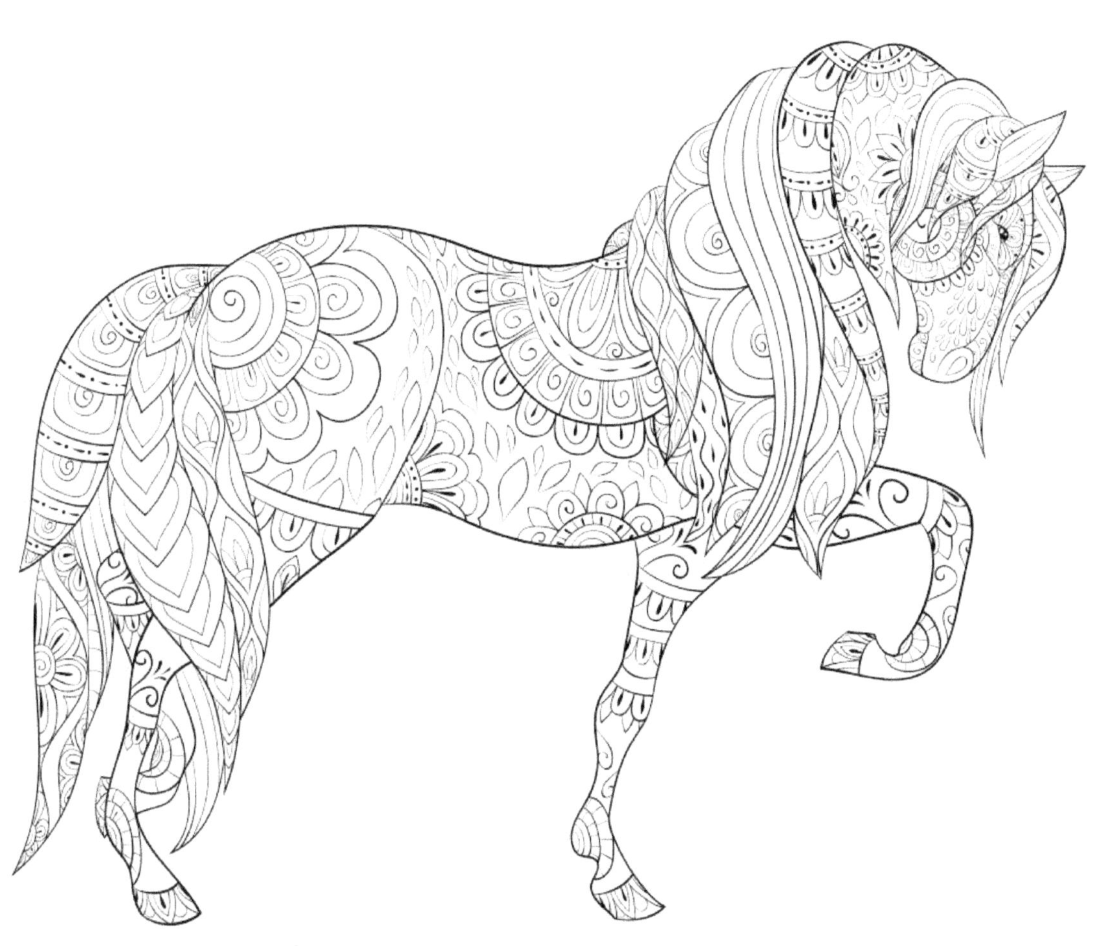

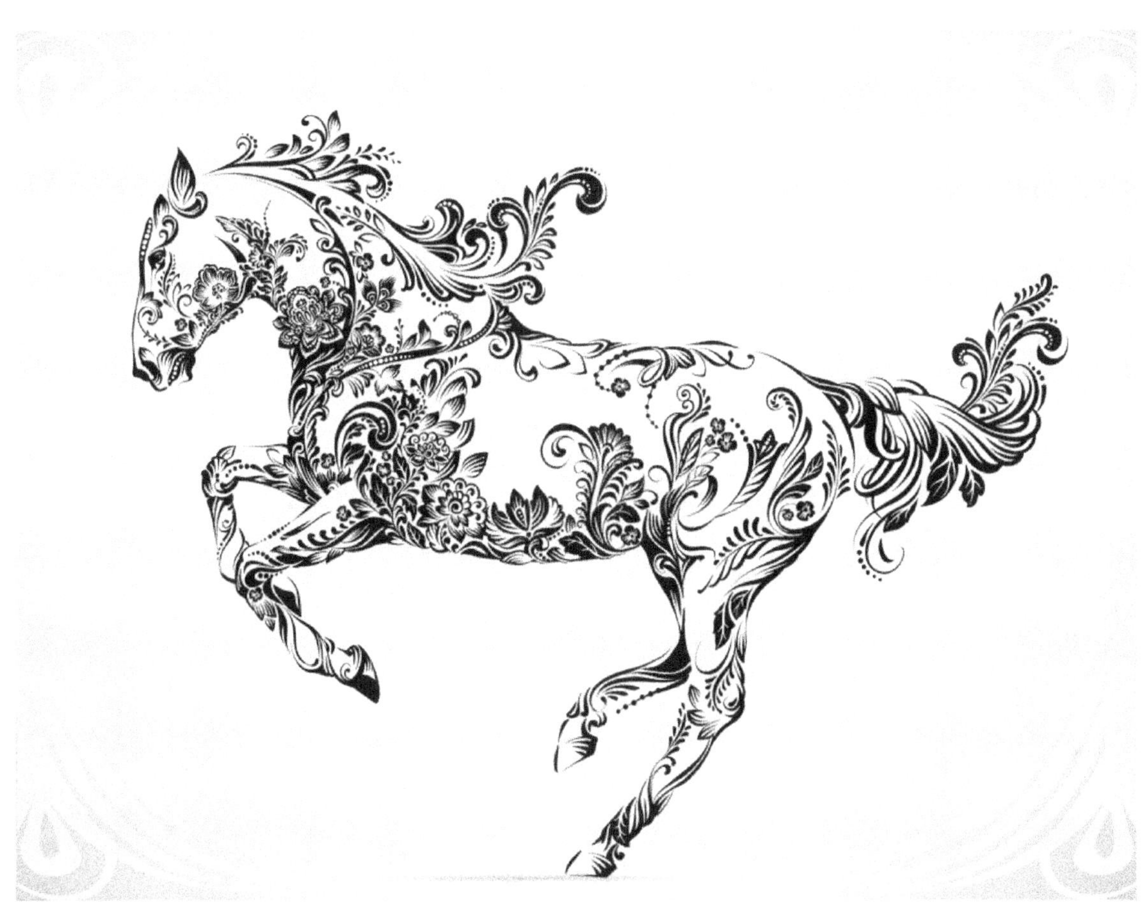

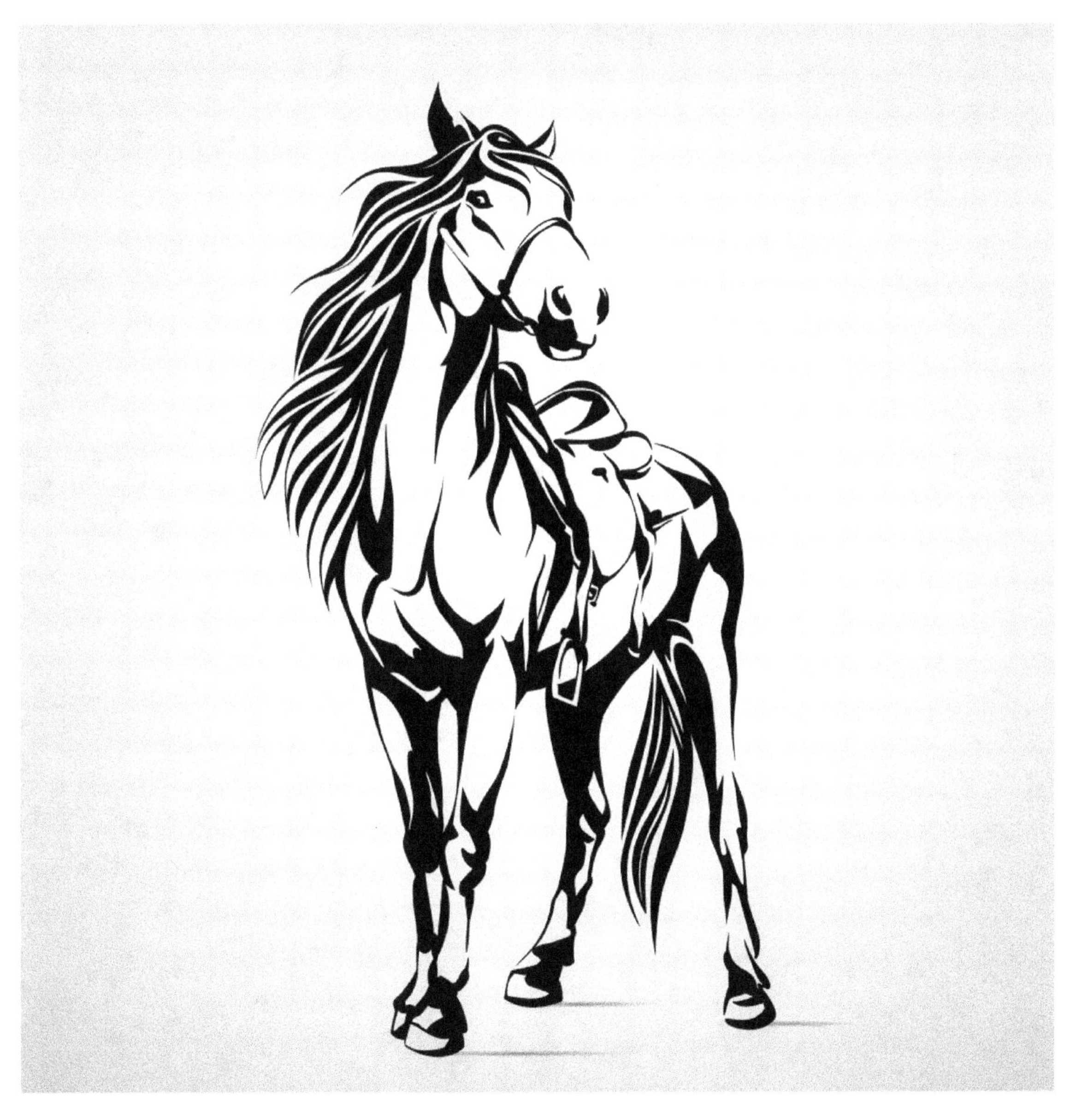

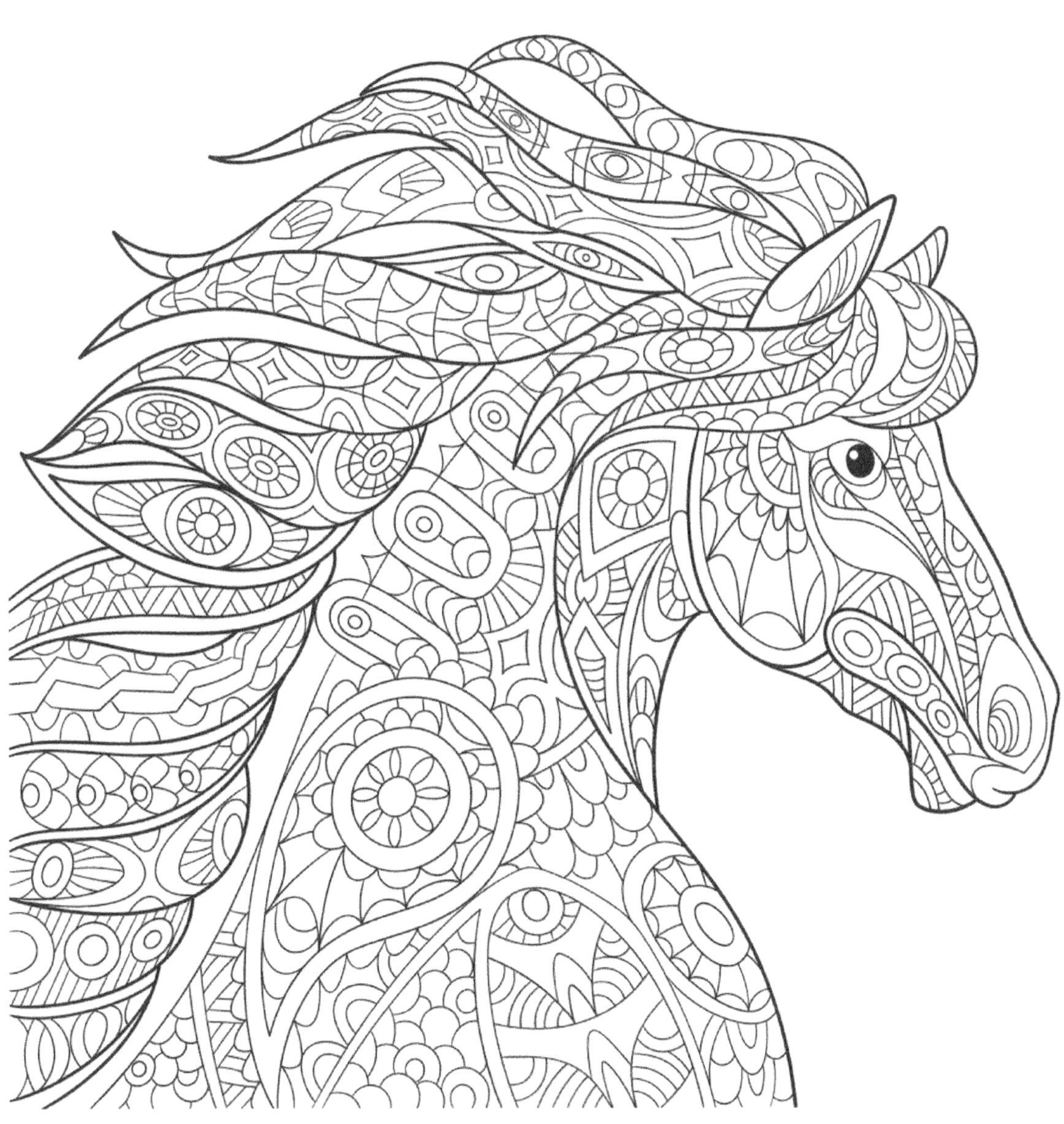

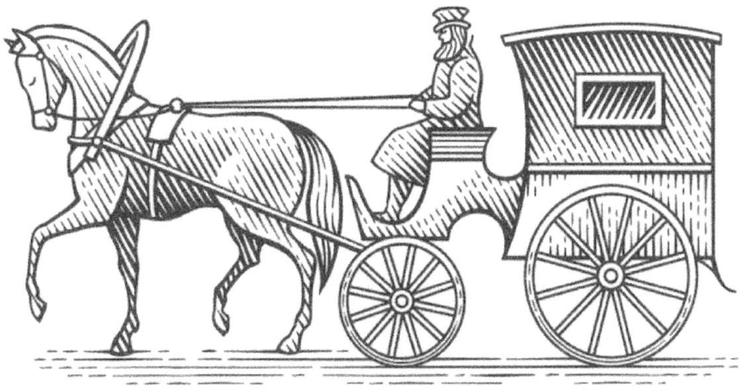

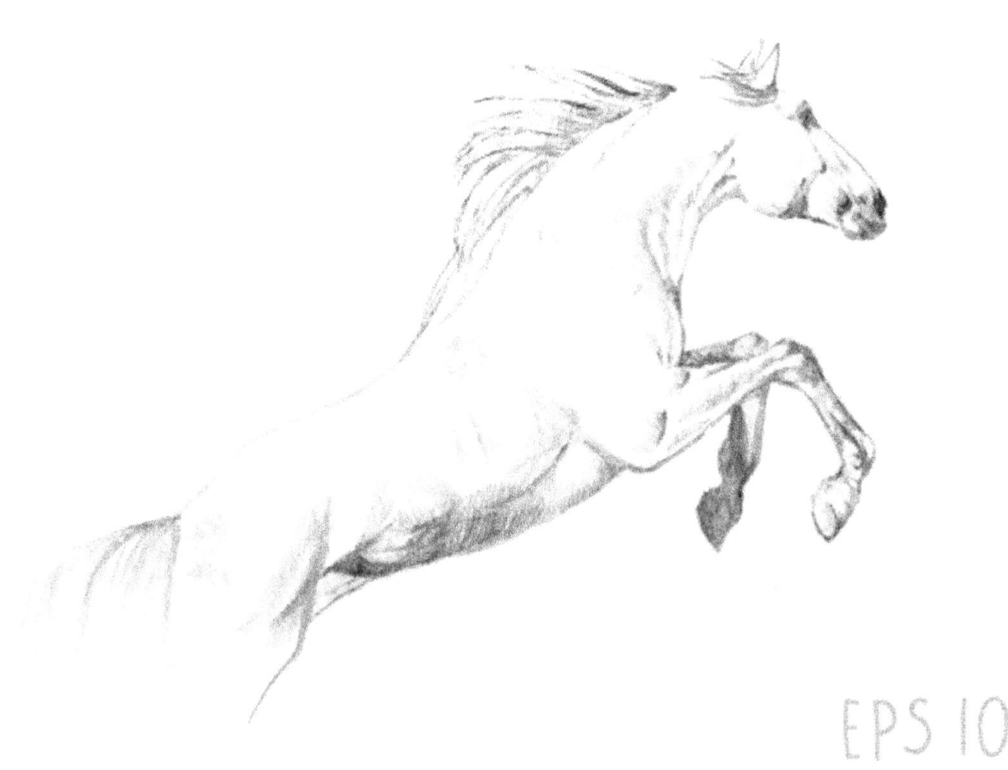

EPS 10

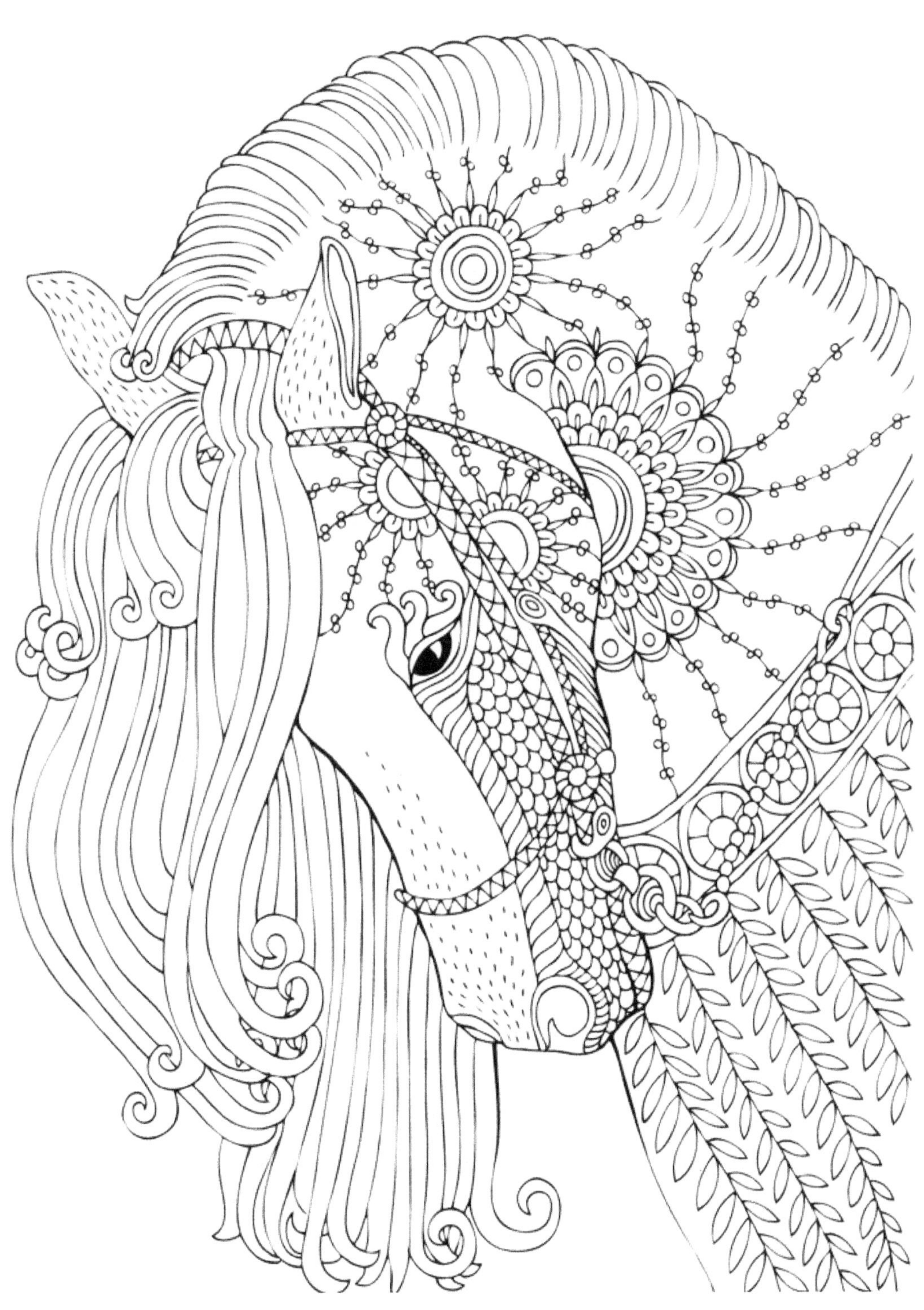

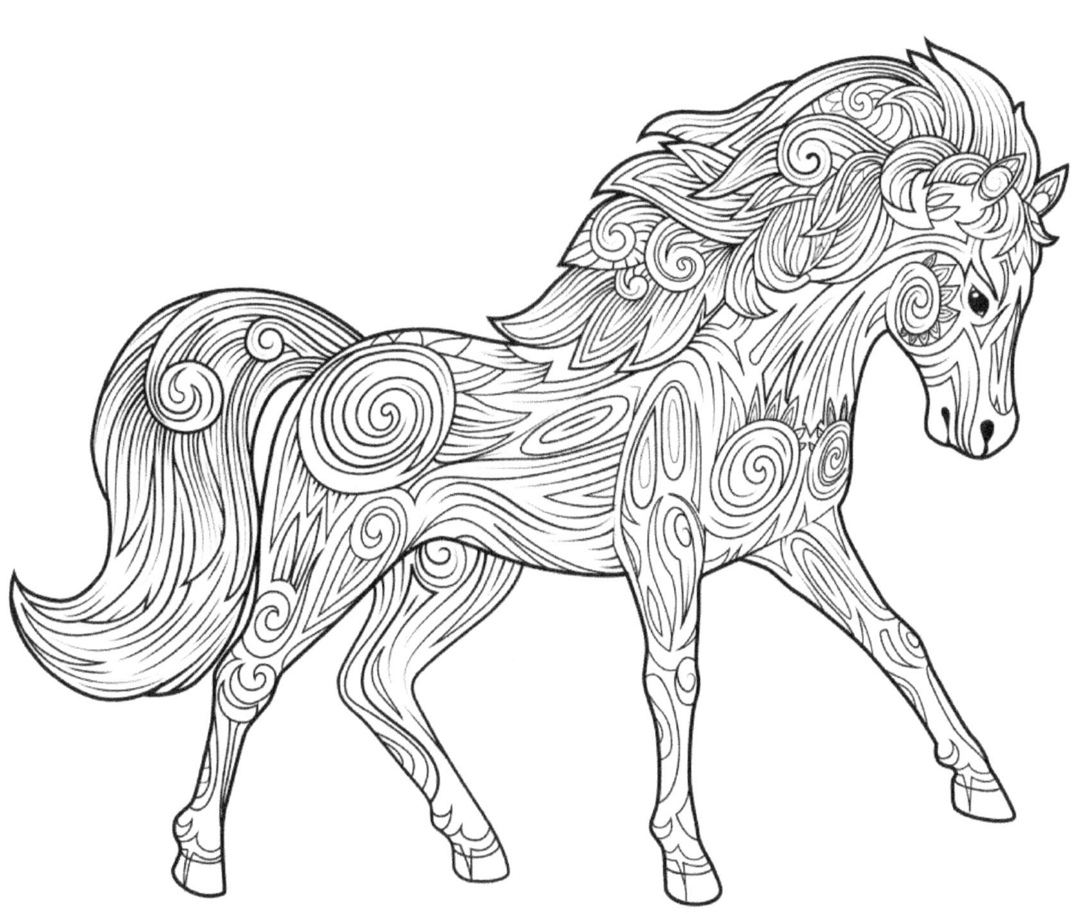

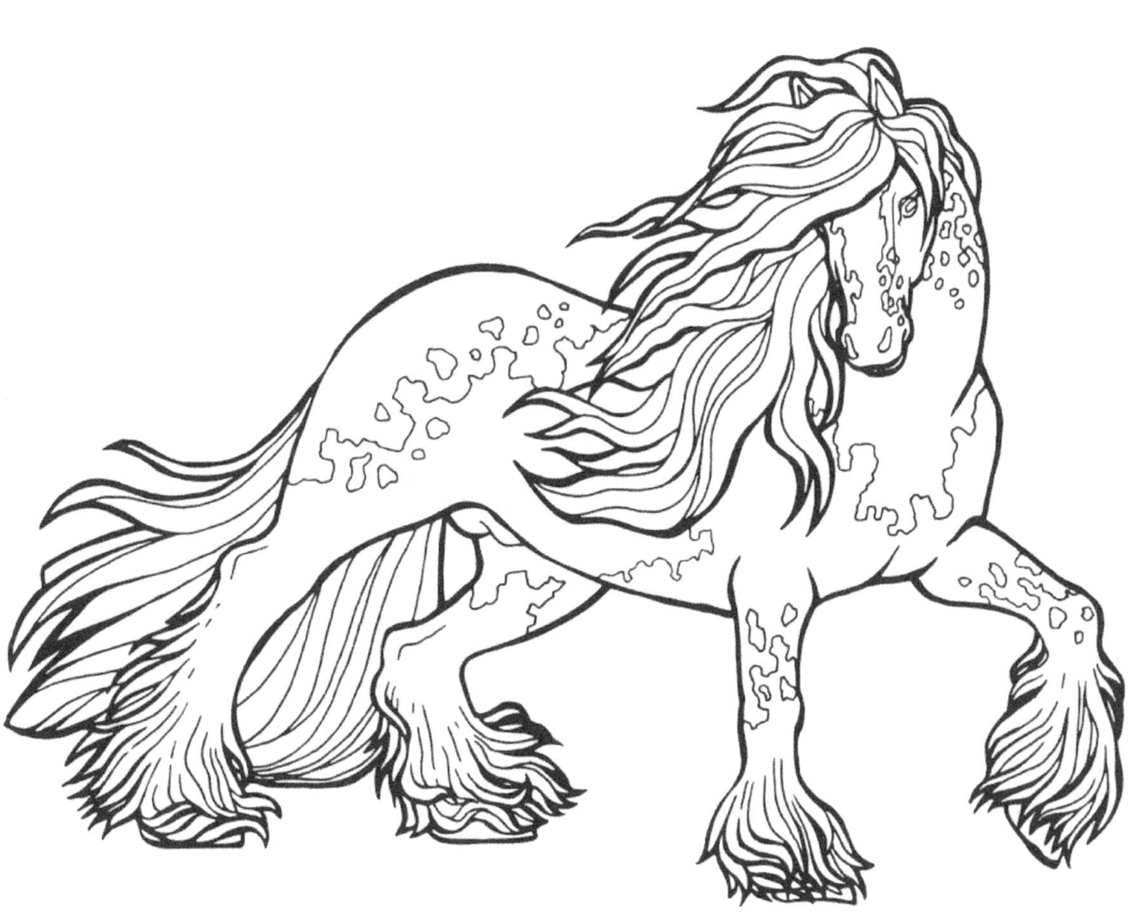

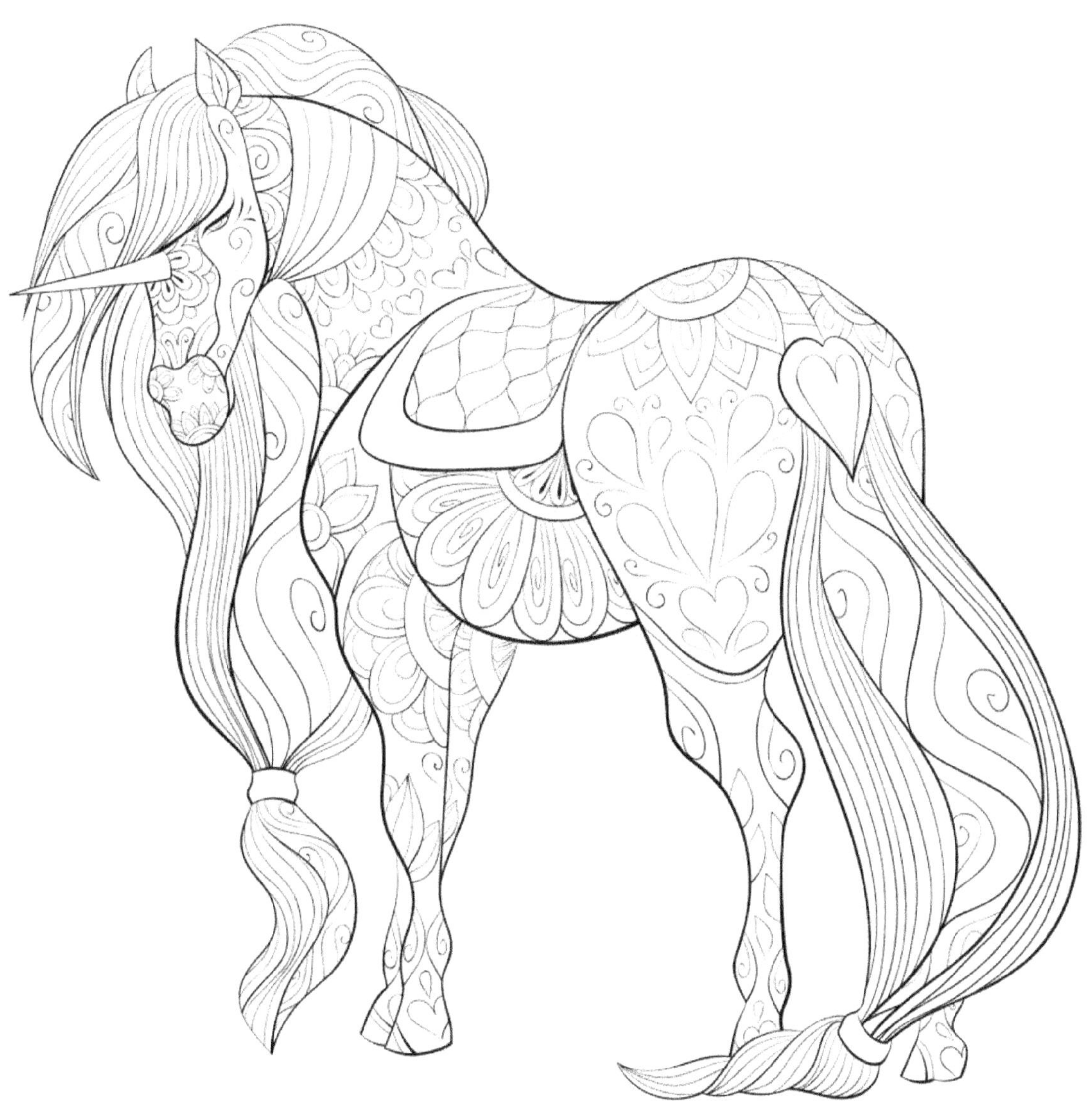

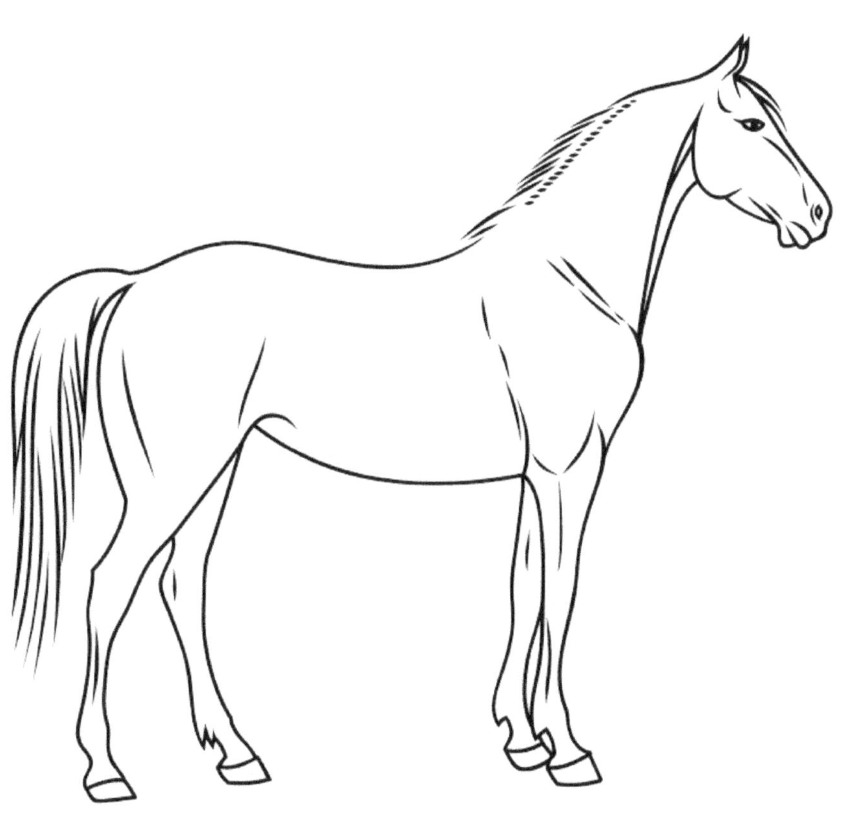

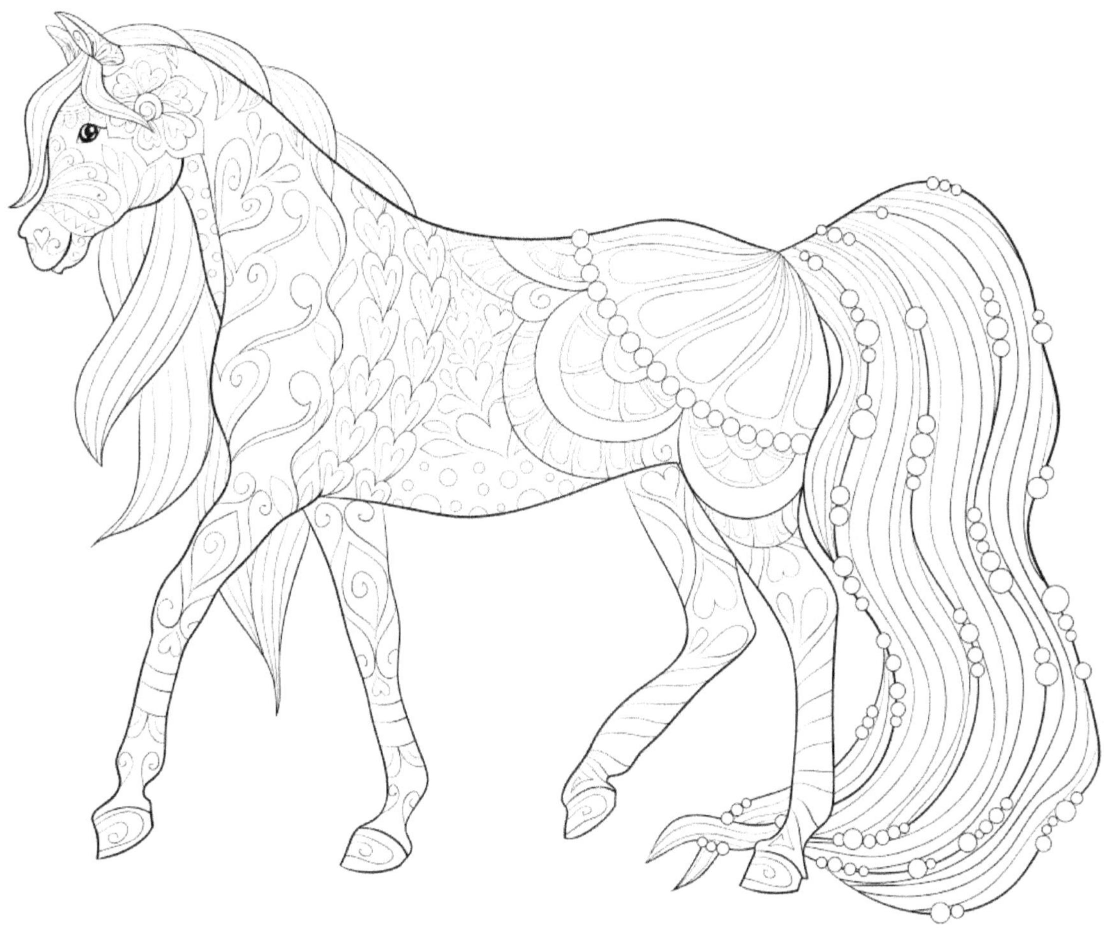

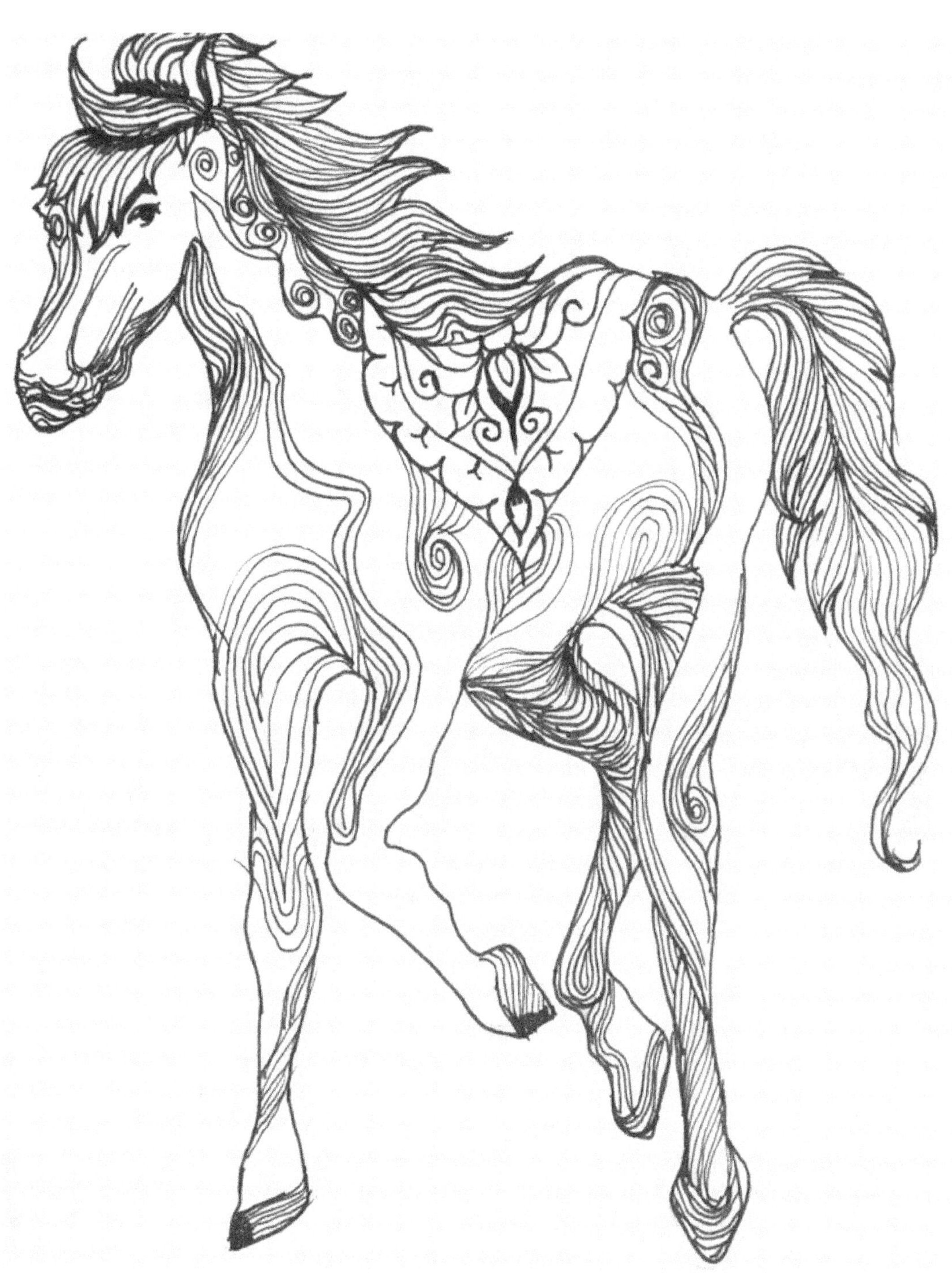

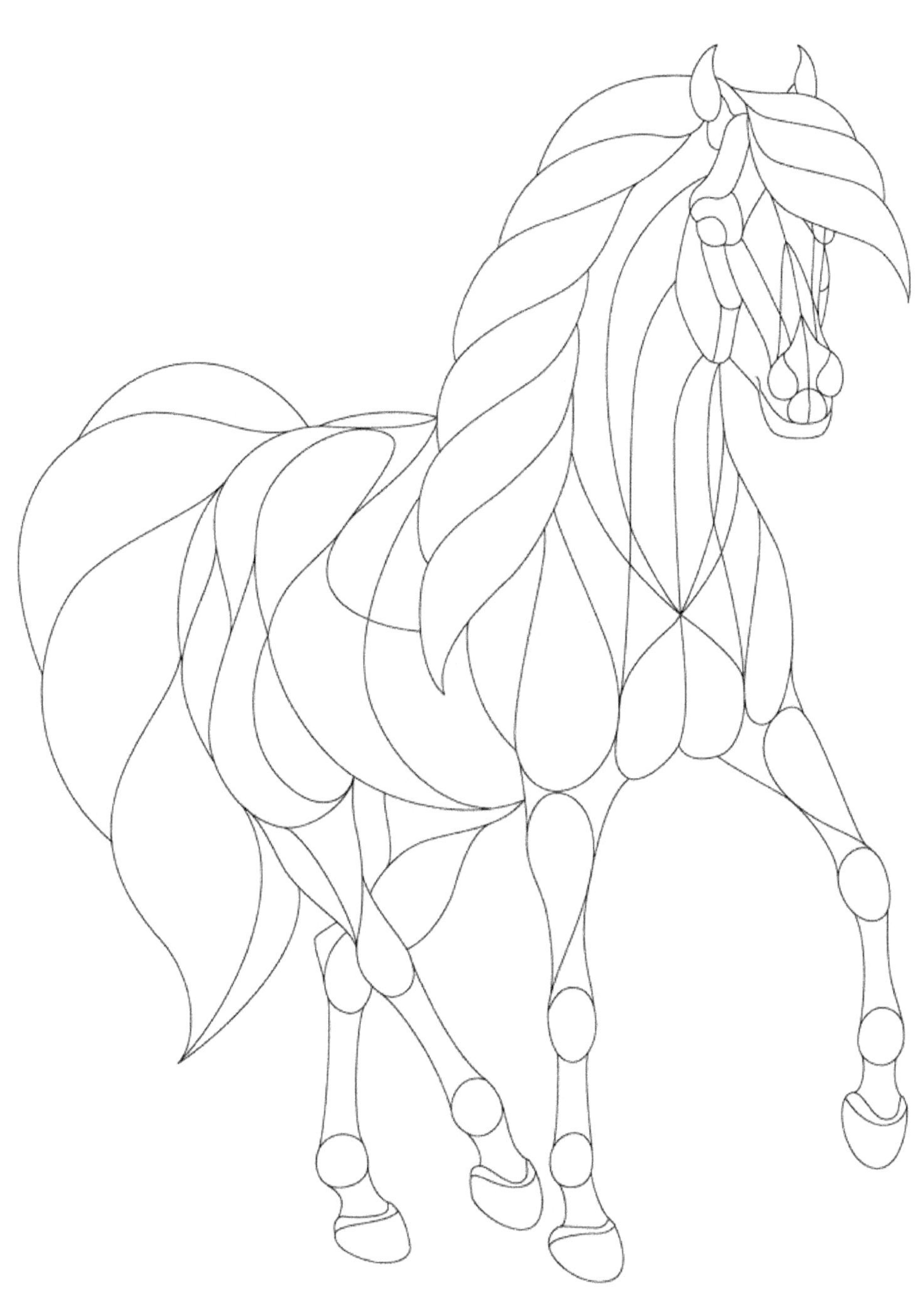

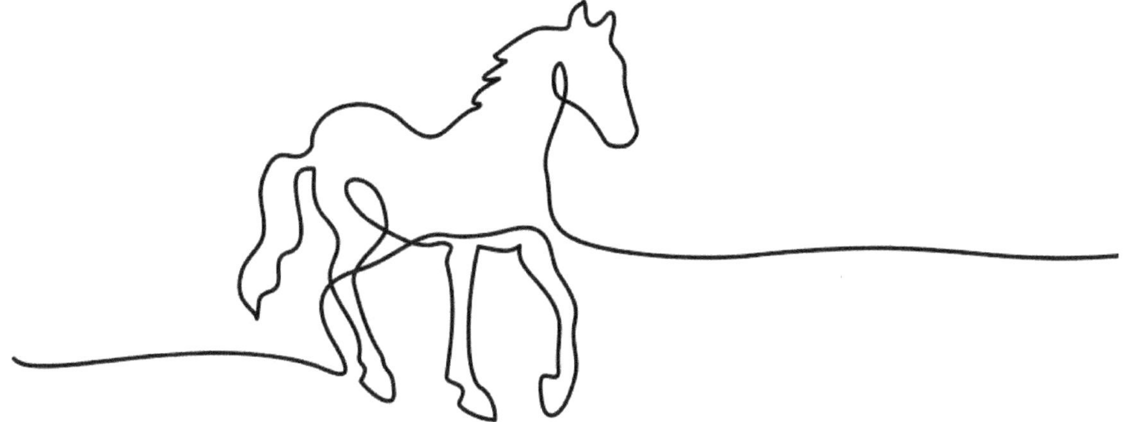

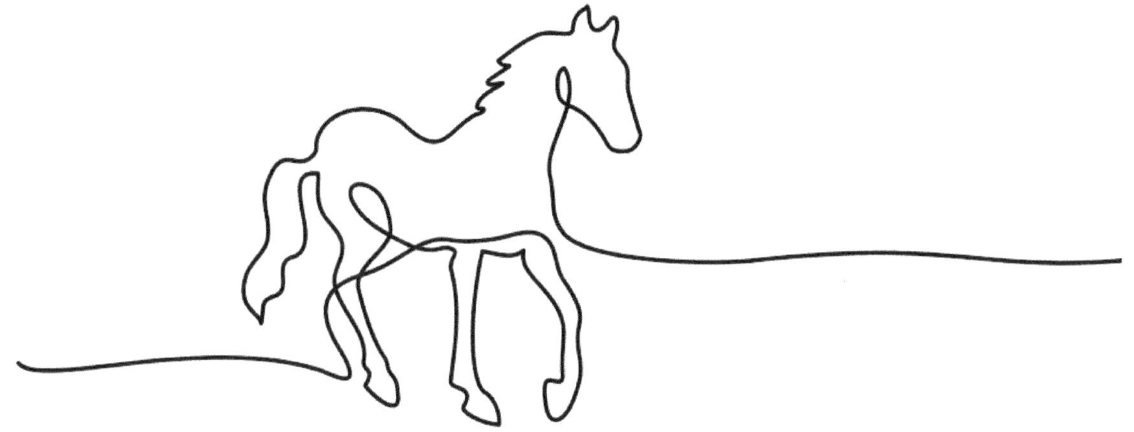

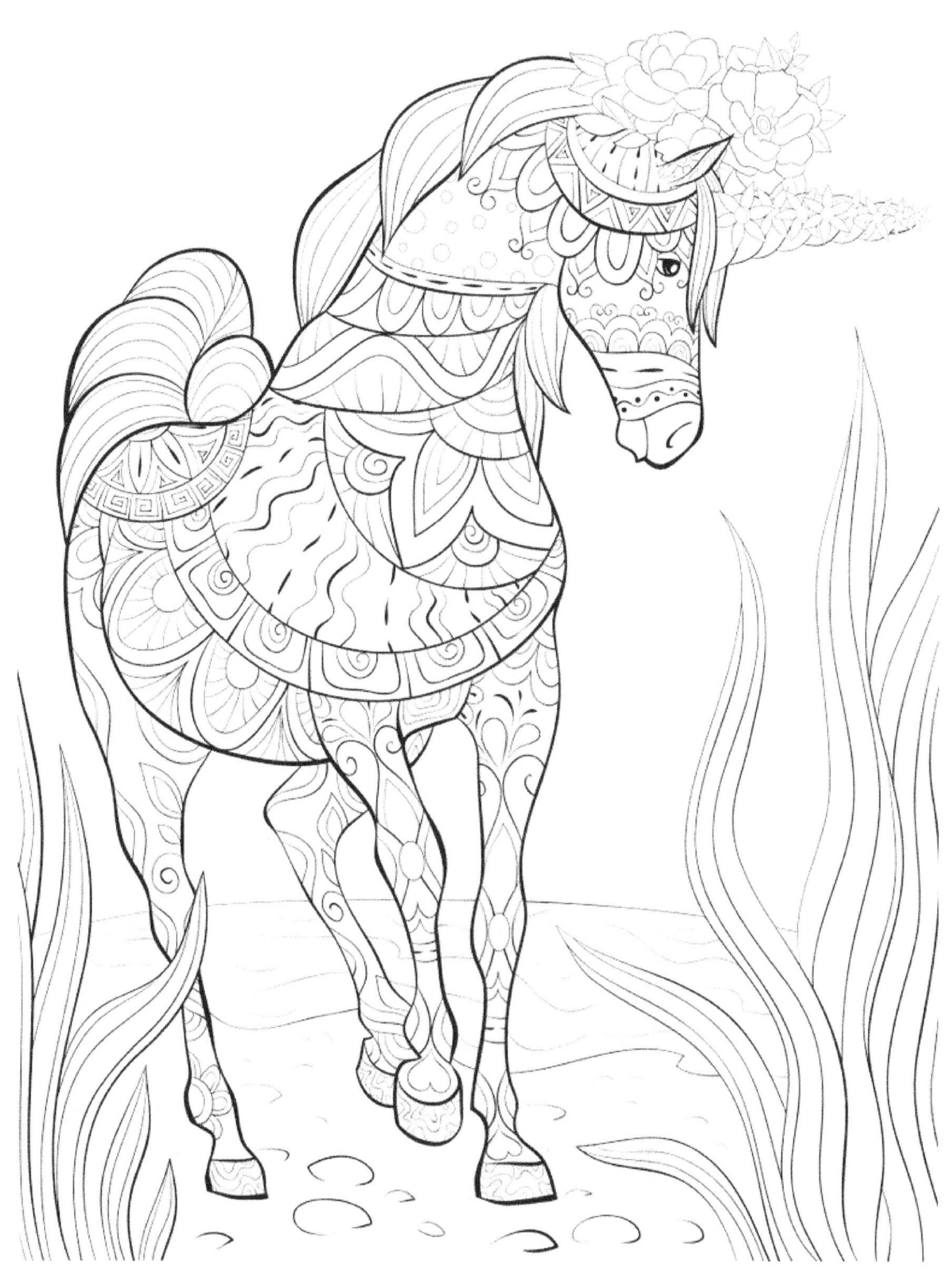

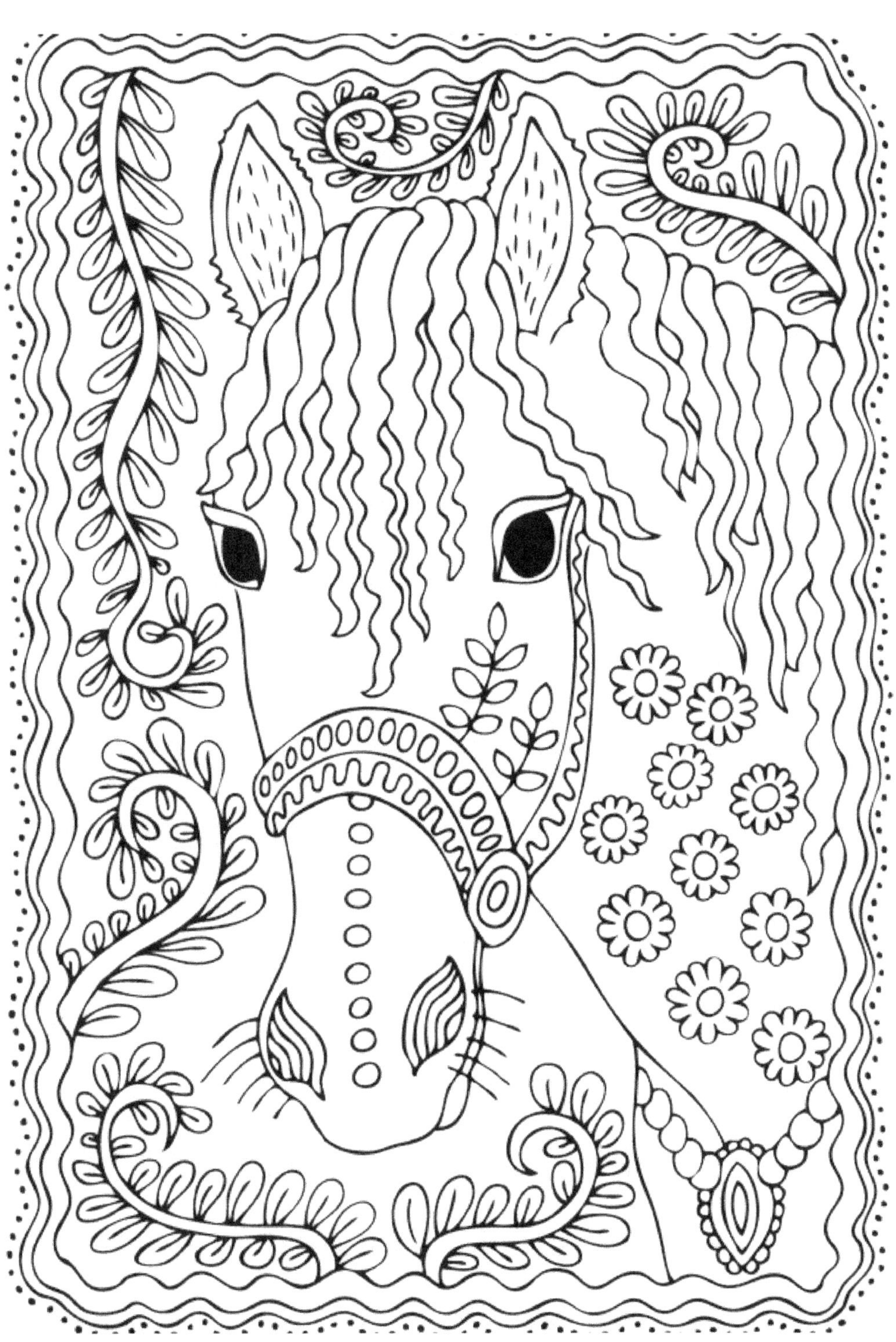